The Disputed Freedoms of a Disrupted Press

The Disputed Freedoms of a Disrupted Press explores the origins, connections, and contradictions evident amongst divergent understandings of press freedom around the world.

Drawing on examples from various countries and cultures, this book distinguishes the universal right of free expression from the more complex and innately conditional liberties claimed by news media. It examines journalists' common goals and norms in light of polarized and disordered information channels, reckonings with identity and privilege, diminished public trust, and altered revenue streams. The author discusses emerging forms of accurate, contextualized news production and argues that journalistic autonomy can be sustained only through demonstrated accountability for providing factual information about public affairs according to self-regulated professional standards. The book concludes by proposing a principle-based framework for enhancing the case for press protections and opposing disinformation while minimizing harm. Adopting this approach would require many publishers and editors to consider paradigm shifts and structural changes.

This is a timely contribution to the body of literature on press freedom and will be a valued resource for advanced students and researchers seeking a contemporary understanding of journalistic practice and the evolving foundations of media law.

Ivor Shapiro is Scholar in Residence at the Centre for Free Expression, Toronto Metropolitan University. He is a former chair of that university's School of Journalism, where he taught narrative reporting as well as media ethics and law until 2020. Shapiro's scholarship on journalists' professional identity and practice has been published in leading international journals and collections and he is an editorial board member of Journalism Studies. Previous roles have included chair of the ethics advisory committee of the Canadian Association of Journalists, principal investigator of the Canadian Worlds of Journalism Study, founding editor of J-Source.ca, managing editor of Chatelaine magazine, and contributing editor of Saturday Night.

Disruptions: Studies in Digital Journalism
Series editor: Bob Franklin

Disruptions refers to the radical changes provoked by the affordances of digital technologies that occur at a pace and on a scale that disrupts settled understandings and traditional ways of creating value, interacting and communicating both socially and professionally. The consequences for digital journalism involve far reaching changes to business models, professional practices, roles, ethics, products and even challenges to the accepted definitions and understandings of journalism. For Digital Journalism Studies, the field of academic inquiry which explores and examines digital journalism, disruption results in paradigmatic and tectonic shifts in scholarly concerns. It prompts reconsideration of research methods, theoretical analyses and responses (oppositional and consensual) to such changes, which have been described as being akin to 'a moment of mind-blowing uncertainty'.

Routledge's book series, *Disruptions: Studies in Digital Journalism*, seeks to capture, examine and analyse these moments of exciting and explosive professional and scholarly innovation which characterize developments in the day-to-day practice of journalism in an age of digital media, and which are articulated in the newly emerging academic discipline of Digital Journalism Studies.

The Disputed Freedoms of a Disrupted Press
Ivor Shapiro

For more information about this series, please visit: www.routledge.com/Disruptions/book-series/DISRUPTDIGJOUR

The Disputed Freedoms of a Disrupted Press

Ivor Shapiro

LONDON AND NEW YORK

First published 2024
by Routledge
4 Park Square, Milton Park, Abingdon, Oxon OX14 4RN

and by Routledge
605 Third Avenue, New York, NY 10158

Routledge is an imprint of the Taylor & Francis Group, an informa business

© 2024 Ivor Shapiro

The right of Ivor Shapiro to be identified as author of this work has been asserted in accordance with sections 77 and 78 of the Copyright, Designs and Patents Act 1988.

All rights reserved. No part of this book may be reprinted or reproduced or utilised in any form or by any electronic, mechanical, or other means, now known or hereafter invented, including photocopying and recording, or in any information storage or retrieval system, without permission in writing from the publishers.

Trademark notice: Product or corporate names may be trademarks or registered trademarks, and are used only for identification and explanation without intent to infringe.

British Library Cataloguing-in-Publication Data
A catalogue record for this book is available from the British Library

Library of Congress Cataloging-in-Publication Data
Names: Shapiro, Ivor, author.
Title: The disputed freedoms of a disrupted press / Ivor Shapiro.
Description: Abingdon, Oxon ; New York : Routledge, 2024. | Series: Disruptions: studies in digital journalism | Includes bibliographical references and index.
Identifiers: LCCN 2023016110 (print) | LCCN 2023016111 (ebook) | ISBN 9781032119977 (hardback) | ISBN 9781032121154 (paperback) | ISBN 9781003223146 (ebook)
Subjects: LCSH: Freedom of the press. | Mass media–Objectivity. | Online journalism–Objectivity.
Classification: LCC PN4736 S54 2024 (print) | LCC PN4736 (ebook) | DDC 323.445–dc23/eng/20230501
LC record available at https://lccn.loc.gov/2023016110
LC ebook record available at https://lccn.loc.gov/2023016111

ISBN: 978-1-032-11997-7 (hbk)
ISBN: 978-1-032-12115-4 (pbk)
ISBN: 978-1-003-22314-6 (ebk)

DOI: 10.4324/9781003223146

Typeset in Times New Roman
by Newgen Publishing UK

This work is
dedicated to
BRIAN MACLEOD ROGERS
friend, teacher,
and lifelong advocate
for a free press
and to
LOUISE PAUL
who soothes my soul
in disrupted times.

Contents

Preface   *xi*

1 The Cost of Liberty   1
  Speech, Disrupted 1
  The Human Rights Revolution 4
  When Words Hurt: The Harm Principle 9
  But, the "Press"? 15

2 Toward a Free Press   16
  The Prisoner's Book 16
  Birth of a Liberty 18
  From Debut to Disruption (A View from South Africa) 21
  Particular Roles, Particular Rights 29

3 The End of The Press That Was   33
  "Good Faith:" The Policing of a Journalist's Mind 33
  Rights Reserved, with Conditions Attached 36
  Privileging a "Qualified" Press (A View from Canada) 39
  Information Disorder and the New "News" 44

4 Shifting Truths, Altered Missions   54
  This, Too, Is News: Journalism's Evolving Shapes 54
  Is That a Fact? Now, It All Depends 59
  Taking Sides with Truth (A View from Argentina) 67
  The Duties That Freedom Demands 71

5 A Profession Whose Time Has Come 77
Where Local News Blooms 77
From Boundary Work to Professional Standards 82
Embracing Accountability (A View From Norway) 88
Facing the Crisis of Trust 92

6 The Precarious Future of a Disrupted Press 97
The Day They Switched Off Journalism 97
News under the Guns (A View from Kashmir) 102
Renewing the Freedom of a Precarious Press 104
What's Worth Fighting For 111

References *114*
Index *141*

Preface

> The people shall govern.... The law shall guarantee to all their right to speak, to organise, to meet together, to publish, to preach, to worship and to educate their children.
> (The Freedom Charter, 1955[1])

> As an army's safety rests in its sentinels, all rights depend on the freedom of the press.
> (Germaine de Staël[2])

I was born in a place ruled by raw power, not law. In those days of apartheid, talking about human rights in South Africa was unacceptable because it made people—White people—feel unsafe. Demanding justice threatened a system that suppressed freedoms of expression, association, and movement for a clear reason: to keep the racialized majority poor and powerless. Black people who spoke out risked beatings, torture, banishment, and detention without trial. Schools taught a highly censored version of history and geography, and people lived in enclaves so homogenous that by comparison today's polarized information channels bustle with diversity.

It was largely thanks to my parents' newspaper subscriptions that I, as a child of privilege, began to learn what was happening in my country and, eventually, began looking over segregation's walls.

1 'The Freedom Charter [Documents on Democracy]'.
2 Author's translation [La liberté de la presse est le seul droit dont tous les autres dépendent; les sentinelles font la sécurité de l'armée.] From de Staël, *Considérations Sur Les Principaux Événemens de La Révolution Française, Ouvrage Posthume*, 1:292.

There, I met mentors and made friends whose experiences were far different from mine. These people took it as a matter of faith that speaking truthfully could alter reality. I learned that talk is not cheap but costly, appreciable, a freedom worth fighting for and treasuring when achieved. I learned to pay speech its due—when talking, to respect its power; when listening, to shut up and ready myself to be moved by the combined force of facts and perspectives.

Those days also taught me a thing or two about "the press" (which, in this book, generally means news media rather than printing machines). Journalists' work under apartheid was highly constrained—by legal limits, by proprietors' caution, and by news workers' own rituals and prejudices. Nevertheless, their efforts frequently exposed the truths. When reporters and photographers attended a peaceful protest, the police seemed to behave a bit better—or at least, when people got hurt or killed, the world noticed. Incomplete and contingent as news reports were (and always are, everywhere[3]), they drew attention to what was going on. Steadily, that attention nourished political opposition and economic pressure. It took decades, but those pressures would eventually help to unlock prison doors and turn a police state into a constitutional democracy.

I offer you, the reader, this personal context, and occasional further such interventions in the following pages, as an acknowledgement that what I think today is inevitably coloured by where I have been over the past seven decades. An especially unsettling example of this personal filter at work came thirty-five years after my immigration to Canada. In September, 2020, a woman named Joyce Echaquan filmed neglect and explicitly racist abuse by staff in a Canadian hospital. She herself was the target, and she was dying even as she touched the "Share" icon. The viral video fuelled news reports and popular outrage—an exhibit of Indigenous people's life realities.[4] I reacted with the same mix of shame and rage as did many others but my inner child of apartheid noted that a private citizen, seizing her constitutionally protected right to communicate with the outside world, had done so to share a terrible truth.

---

3 See Carey, 'Why and How'.
4 Cecco, 'Canada: Outcry after Video Shows Hospital Staff Taunting Dying Indigenous Woman'.

The power of truth-telling is that it lets people see their world more clearly and sometimes helps them change it. Almost all political change-making consists largely of people talking (or yelling, or picketing, or gluing themselves to things, or blocking streets) and of people listening or talking or yelling (*et cetera*) back. When power is at stake, talk is seldom polite and never easy, but the only alternatives—silence and violence—are worse. When people make themselves heard, good things can happen. And when they do, freedom of speech deserves some credit.

That is the relatively simple starting point of a more complicated journey on which I hope you'll accompany me, in the pages ahead, through the following main waypoints.

Chapter 1 locates the idea of freedom of expression within the broad frame of human rights. It briefly explores the ancient origins of these concepts, their modern development in constitutional law, and the challenges that "free speech" faces in an era characterized by heavily filtered information channels and lies disguised as facts. It introduces the "harm principle" as a widely accepted method of placing necessary constraints on speech freedom.

Chapter 2 moves from expression in general to the beginnings, implications, and essential contributions of the press. It traces the beginnings of journalism and censorship and explores how journalism has claimed a growing range of reserved rights and privileges. These claims have been justified by a distinct social responsibility: to gather and provide accurate information about current affairs.

Chapter 3 shows how the disruption of news channels has diminished news-media pluralism (a vital aspect of press freedom) and undermined journalists' and publishers' claims to legal entitlements. Meanwhile, calls for various kinds of censorship have been bolstered by the difficulty of distinguishing journalists from marketers and propagandists, and, more generally, sorting truth from lies.

Chapter 4 probes the viability of traditional arguments for journalistic privilege in an era characterized by diverging forms and norms amid a worldwide reckoning with identity-based assumptions. While journalists bring preformed assumptions to bear on their work, accepting full-on "standpoint epistemology" is irreconcilable with claiming press privileges. Traditional appeals to high-minded concepts such as monitoring power and maintaining detachment are less useful to this claim than fulfilling the core responsibility of providing accurate information.

Chapter 5 introduces notions of "professional" standards for journalists and shows how a crisis in audience trust may expose gaps between claimed autonomy and recognized accountability. Despite many kinds of diversity, journalists and stakeholders are not far from agreement on foundational goals and standards, but robust structures of self-regulation are less common than performative brand-enhancement measures.

The sixth and final chapter projects a precarious future for press entitlements. The privileges and constraints of news media have grown too complex to be mounted on journalists' and publishers' pre-disruption assumptions. Radical changes will be needed in some areas to replenish public support for truth-telling on current affairs. The book ends with a list of post-disruption changes that might help to break the impasse over press freedom.

Each chapter except the first includes an intercontinental reporting expedition that grounds my developing argument in real-life exigencies. Chapter 2 describes the evolution of a free monitorial press in South Africa from colonial times through White nationalist rule to the current democratic era. Chapter 3 moves (as I did, in 1985) from Africa to North America; it describes features of Canada's controversial regulatory efforts to designate some information providers for publicly funded support and legal privileges. Chapter 4 visits a pioneering fact-checking outlet in Argentina to explore the viability of truth-telling as a continuing journalistic purpose, and Chapter 5 heads to Norway, testing ideas of professional accountability against national self-regulation and local practice in a small community newspaper. The final chapter tracks a young Kashmiri journalist's evolving career under the guns of India's union government.

The book's inception lay in a suggestion from the *Disruptions* series editor, Bob Franklin, who had, for many years previous, gently mitigated my imposter worries and encouraged my sometimes esoteric investigations of journalists' professional identity and norms of practice, as did Abby Goodrum, Brian Gabrial, Charles Davis, Folker Hanusch, Gene Allen, Herman Wasserman, Jody Jacobson, Kim Sawchuk, Paul Knox, Thomas Hanitzsch, and the late John Honderich.

Preface xv

Jim Turk, director of the Centre for Free Expression at Toronto Metropolitan University, provided invaluable advice and support for this book, portions of which first appeared as blog posts on the Centre's website. My work in this subject area has leaned heavily on the advice and insights of Colette Brin, Heather Rollwagen, Lisa Taylor, and co-investigators including Patrizia Albanese, Martín Oller Alonso, Geneviève Bonin, George Gladney, Lee Marshall, Philippa Spoel, Asmaa Malik, and Kasia Mychajlowycz. Key insights, connections, or encouragement were offered by Kenneth Andresen, Nick Benequista, Nicole Blanchett, Geoff Budlender, Jamie Cameron, Menán du Plessis, Farid Esack, Sonya Fatah, Lindsay Fitzgerald, Ryder Gilliland, Edward Greenspon, Bernie Lucht, Alain Musikanth, Janice Neil, Kim Pittaway, Brian MacLeod Rogers, Sarmishta Subramanian, and Chris Waddell.

The "view from Kashmir" in Chapter 6 was reported by Rajalaxmi Nayak. Aloysius Wong led a dream team of research assistants that included Brit Weaver, Christin El-Kholy, and the aforementioned Rajalaxmi Nayak. Howard Law provided invaluable policy context on several key aspects of this book's argument. Carlien and Jannie Fourie were kind and patient with my eccentric hours and poor clarinet-playing during my writing retreat under their roof in Cape Town. David Shapiro provided encouragement while keeping me somewhat humble. Louise Paul was the chief pre-submission copyeditor before the manuscript was handed off to the superbly professional publishing staff at Routledge/Taylor & Francis in London, where my work has often been improved over past years; many thanks to Elizabeth Cox and her colleague Hannah McKeating for assigning and editing this book.

Deepest thanks of all are due to those who gave time to be interviewed for this book: Adil Amin Akhoon, Anton Harber, Arne Jensen, Berit Rekaa, Brent Jolly, Elin Floberghagen, Guilherme Canela de Souza Godoi, Guy Berger, Hege Iren Frantzen, Iram Ansari, Janne B. Prestvold, Kristoffer Egeberg, Laura Zommer, Marcelo Rech, Martin Gundersen, Olivia Sohr, Paul Bjerke, Paul Deegan, Rune Ottosen, Sigurd Haugsgjerd (and Olav Haugsgjerd, who translated for us), Stefaans Brümmer, Stein Bjøntegård, and Vidya Kauri.

Toronto: January, 2023

1 The Cost of Liberty

Abstract

The right to speak freely is much disputed and misunderstood at a time when disrupted information channels foster polarization, distrust, deception, and open hatred. This chapter locates the notion of free expression within the broad frame of human rights—the idea that all people deserve to be treated fairly. The idea's roots lay in diverse ancient traditions, became codified in national constitutions after liberal revolutions, and entered international treaties as a desired antidote to world wars. Rights charters feature prominent guarantees of freedom of speech. This fundamental freedom underpins human dignity and democratic participation but also carries destructive potential. It has, therefore, long been considered subject to reasonable limits under the so-called harm principle, whose scope continues to be debated and refined. News media ("the press") have won additional legal protections whose purposes and increasing challenges will be investigated in following chapters.

Speech, Disrupted

Consider each of the following sentences. Is it true, false, or a matter of opinion?

> Freedom of expression distracts people from addressing urgent social issues.
> Freedom of expression helps people solve urgent social problems.

DOI: 10.4324/9781003223146-1

End-to-end encryption of social messaging allows terrorists and other criminals to plot in secret.

Qualified and reputable researchers dispute the effectiveness of conventional responses to pandemics and climate change.

Regulation and moderation of social media platforms reduce the harm done by online content.

A necessary exchange of perspectives requires universities to treat all student groups alike, including those that either support or oppose abortion rights and gender equality.

Governments' financial aid for news organizations protects the free flow of knowledge about public affairs.

Cartoons depicting the prophet Mohammed are a type of hate speech.

The following statement is hate speech: "Zionists must pay the price of the Palestinians' suffering."

Universities should prevent students' involuntary exposure to class materials that make them feel unsafe.

Universities should provide secure forums for anyone to express an opinion on public affairs.

No two readers are likely to agree on all of the above statements. Where we come from, where we live, who we are, and what we and our friends believe will all affect our assessments. Now, more than ever.

This century's first two decades saw collisions in many parts of the world between two seemingly equal and opposite cultural forces: a growing resistance to the force of systemic racism and other forms of social and economic discrimination, and widespread populist mobilizations of people who see themselves as disempowered by inclusiveness.

In the same period, many people's ideas about public affairs, in general, have become so polarized that we each tune in mainly to information channels that our friends share, a habit that feeds our existing assumptions (that is, prejudices) rather than exposing us to new or different perspectives. That's not good—but it's made far worse by the large number of people who derive gratification and/or profit from crafting and spreading well-disguised lies (false news) on the internet.[1]

---

1 Wardle and Derakhshan, 'Information Disorder', 29–38.

A particular collision point among people who disagree about public issues has been their different understandings of free expression (or, informally, free "speech"). This classically liberal idea has become so frequently avowed by right-wing populists that many progressives feel compelled to distance themselves from it. Some demand that free expression should yield to other, more urgent human needs: the freedom to eat, for example, to have a home, and to live safely. So long as people enjoy disparate shares of social, economic and political freedoms, it's understandable that those less privileged tire of hearing complaints about pressures for ideological uniformity, often termed as "cancel culture."

The commotion of extremes drowns more nuanced voices: those who see democratic value in free speech while *also* viewing racist speech as innately harmful; those who fight racism while *also* believing that where dissenting views are silenced, tyranny will thrive.

Nor should this blurry snapshot of today's word-wars obscure a centuries-long history of disputes over the boundaries of discourse. It's always been true that one person's truth, insight, or experience is another's lie, hope, or hate, but digital information channels have proven so polarized and all-consuming that new assertions of fact are more easily parsed for familiarity than for reliability. The more frequently I feel ambushed and assaulted by my news feed, the less inclined I will be to see new information as both surprising and factual; I'll stop following the most upsetting stuff and thus prevent new facts, alleged facts, and opinions from affecting my life choices. To break this habit of thought requires more effort with every passing year. Meanwhile, successful politicians can be forgiven for shaping policy options to your or my artificially manipulated prejudices rather than to evidence-based solutions to urgent problems.

As for *freedom of speech* and its cousin, *freedom of the press*, these notions, too, have become increasingly upsetting. Discussing them is now so complicated and divisive that some people find them unnecessary distractions from what matters more. Sure, these things were important, in their day, but with so much else to argue over, do they still deserve so prominent a space on the menu of human rights?

It's a fair question.

The Human Rights Revolution

The idea of legally protecting human rights rests on an ancient and transcultural assumption that people deserve to be treated fairly "for no other reason than that they constitute integral moral beings."[2]

For millennia, solidarity with a universal human race has been an item of faith in Confucianism, Buddhism, and Hinduism as well as many interpretations of Jewish, Christian, and Muslim belief, and it gained a philosophical structure in the Stoicism of Greece and Rome. Indigenous traditions promoted human rights from the realm of morals and beliefs to legal protections; Shelley Wright has described, for example, how the Asante culture in Ghana encompasses human rights guaranteed in an "elaborate system of constitutional checks and balances" that developed long before European contact.[3] In ancient Asia, Babylon's Code of Hammurabi promised access to justice and "progressive punishment."[4]

Over the millennia, as people explored new valleys, wandered continents, and crossed oceans, they shared some of their foods, their skills, and beliefs with those strangers they didn't exterminate. Among the ideas being spread were notions we now collect under the heading of human rights,[5] a "shifting... transnationally defined entity" that was, in Anthony Chase's words:

> often rearticulated and redeployed in different contexts, making the search for a point of origin misleading. It is intellectually impoverished to conceptualize human rights as eternally defined by one historic moment that has since progressed in a linear fashion. The key to human rights' relevance (or lack thereof), instead, has been the way its permutations respond (or do not respond) to the needs of peoples around the globe.[6]

---

2 Reus-Smit, 'Human Rights in a Global Ecumene'.
3 Wright, *International Human Rights, Decolonisation and Globalisation*, 37.
4 Ishay, *The History of Human Rights*, 7.
5 See also Headley, *The Europeanization of the World*, 66–72; Perelló, 'On Supernatural Law'.
6 Chase, 'The Transnational Muslim World, Human Rights, and the Rights of Women and Sexual Minorities', 11.

It is as if, across millennia of occasional contacts, peoples shared droplets of hope in humanity that gathered into trickles, creeks, and eventual rivers of nascent opposition to tyranny and bigotry. Then came the eighteenth-century revolutionary floods, and the dams of liberal declarations behind which nations may drink from shared lakes of constitutional law.[7]

The Age of Constitutions

"Men are born and remain free and equal in rights," declared the French revolutionaries in 1789, and: "Social distinctions may be founded only upon the general good."[8] This proposition, that universal rights could supersede a country's laws, crossed an epistemological border equivalent to anatomy's blood-brain barrier. Certainly, it blew the minds of many born to privilege, such as the English philosopher, Jeremy Bentham, who famously sniffed that the revolutionary French idea of "natural and imprescriptible rights" was:

> ...nonsense upon stilts. But this rhetorical nonsense ends in the old strain of mischievous nonsense: for immediately a list of these pretended natural rights is given, and those are so expressed as to present to view legal rights.[9]

But the nonsense stuck. A key development came with the advent of what Germans call a Basic Law—a more intuitive term for what's known elsewhere as a national constitution. These formal constraints on states' powers began as dubious bargains between European rulers and the tax-paying *bourgeoisie* but, as democracies blossomed, liberals successively won the addition of bills of rights to their countries' super-laws. Governments now owed duties to their citizens—first applied to White men only, and then to women, slaves, and the subjects of colonial regimes. Kings surrendered to parliaments, and a path was beaten toward a day when "heathen" beliefs, traditions, and families would be released from Christian hegemony.

---

7 See Headley, *The Europeanization of the World*.
8 'Declaration of the Rights of Man - 1789' Article 1.
9 Bentham, 'Anarchical Fallacies', 60 (article II).

It took transcontinental wars and anticolonial uprisings for constitutional liberties to cross a final great divide—that from national to international law. Latin American leaders in the 1930s, building on three centuries of campaigns in that region against slavery and for Indigenous people's rights, paved a path to the world's first international rights agreements.[10] In 1938, the Pan American Union gathered in Lima to pledge interstate peace and affirm new freedoms for women and workers, amongst others.[11] The Lima agreement also condemned racial and religious persecution, established an inter-American court to resolve disputes and ensure "the free exercise of rights," and declared that "freedom of expression of thought in all its forms is a necessary and logical consequence" of workers' rights.[12]

After another world war came another peace, and once again it was Latin American delegates to the infant United Nations who joined European idealists to push for inclusion of an international bill of rights in the UN's founding documents. The idea took hold, and the new body's division for education, science, and culture, UNESCO, got right on the project in the way international organizations do: slowly.

The founding director-general, British evolutionary biologist and renowned humanist Julian Huxley invited about 150 writers, thinkers and politicians to offer suggestions that would, he hoped, unearth international consensus for, as he put it, a "unified and unifying background of thought for the modern world." Of approximately fifty-five responses, six were received from the Soviet Union, three from India, two from Latin America, one from an English woman, one from a Chinese consultant to UNESCO, and the rest from White men of European origin.[13] Mahatma Gandhi, writing while on a train to the newly independent India's capital, Delhi, pleaded lack of time for a full response and claimed to be a "poor reader," but offered this advice:

---

10 Lorca, 'Human Rights in International Law?', 476; Glendon, 'The Forgotten Crucible', 32–34.
11 Glendon, 'The Forgotten Crucible', 28–32.
12 Pan American Union, *Report on the Results of the Conference*, 55–64 (resolutions VIII, XX, XXV, XXVI, and XXXVI).
13 Goodale, 'The Myth of Universality'.

I learnt from my illiterate but wise mother that all rights to be deserved and preserved came from duty well done. Thus, the very right to live accrues to us, only when we do the duty of citizenship to the world. From this one fundamental statement, perhaps it is easy enough to define the duties of Man and Woman and correlate every right to some corresponding duty to be first seen performed. Every other right can be shown to be a usurpation hardly worth fighting for.[14]

Gandhi was not the only respondent to suggest a link between rights and obligations, a complex idea that later chapters will revisit. Other correspondence represented a range of liberal, communist, and social-democratic approaches to the topic; various philosophical and scientific approaches; Christian, Muslim, and Hindu perspectives; and considerations of the specific rights of children, prisoners, and "primitive" peoples. A detailed consideration of Confucian and other Chinese traditions included an ancient "right of the people to revolt against oppressive rulers."[15]

Some respondents were critical of the entire project—none more so than the poet and author, T.S. Eliot, who considered it impossible that any such international statement could command global assent unless it were a "tissue of ambiguities."[16] Nevertheless, the *Universal Declaration of Human Rights* was adopted in 1948 by all UN members except eight authoritarian states (six in the Soviet bloc plus Saudi Arabia and segregationist South Africa). It affirms "the inherent dignity and... equal and inalienable rights of all members of the human family," who are thereby entitled to life, liberty, work, leisure, education, belief, peaceful assembly and association, judicial process, and a host of other rights including expression plus freedom from slavery, torture, arbitrary arrest, and enforced marriages.[17]

Any state seeking UN membership must assent to the *Universal Declaration* and all but a few have also bound themselves by treaty to various other conventions on the civil or economic rights of

---

14 Goodale, *Letters to the Contrary*, 119.
15 Goodale, 182.
16 Goodale, 330.
17 'Universal Declaration of Human Rights'.

people in general or various subsets (such as women, children, and people living with disabilities).[18] Most countries also formally defer to substantially similar regional treaties under which governments' actions can be adjudicated by national and international courts. Meanwhile, the language of human rights continues to evolve outside the realm of constitutional law thanks to the influence of oral traditions (e.g., that strangers have a right to be welcomed) and newer teachings (such as John Rawls's explanation of natural justice as blind-to-self-interest consideration of conflicting needs, the feminist ethics of care founded by Carol Gilligan, and many others).

And yet, human rights continue to be flouted repeatedly, openly, and defiantly in most countries on all continents.

Some government leaders ignore reminders of their treaty obligations or are litigated into reluctant compliance; others claim exemptions due to differences between local faith or culture and liberal Northern or Western traditions. When China was condemned by international human-rights groups for slaughtering pro-democracy protestors in 1989, it responded that the entire project of human rights amounted to Western imperialism, a form of argument often echoed in appeals to Asian or African "values" or religious strictures.[19] For example, when the United Nations Convention on the Elimination of All Forms of Discrimination Against Women was agreed in 1979, several countries signed with "reservations" that effectively excused themselves from implementing Article 2, which guarantees full equality between women and men.[20] As Morocco's note of reservation put it, Sharia law provides different rights to women and men "to strike a balance between the spouses in order to preserve the coherence of family life."[21]

The many exceptions and excuse-us notes concerning specific rights make it hard to score the contributions of national and international charters. Yet, Patrick Macklem offers a reminder that the treaties provide a "vocabulary of justice" that helps people to:

---

18 'Status of Ratification: Interactive Dashboard'.
19 Goodale, 'The Myth of Universality', 597.
20 Convention on the Elimination of All Forms of Discrimination against Women.
21 'Declarations, Reservations, Objections…', 22.

...distinguish legal acts from arbitrary violence and coercion. Human rights frame the moral, shape the political, and distinguish the legal in places as local and diverse as the family, the school, the workplace the community, the nation, and the State. But their true significance lies in their status as international legal entitlements that call for radical revision of the ways in which international law organizes global politics into an international legal order.[22]

It is a bold claim that the "true significance" of human rights lies in their status as law. The opposite could be true—that the idea of universal rights and freedom is a kind of ontological myth or all-embracing "story" that we humans have come to tell ourselves as a way of justifying an array of expectations in a harsh world. Either way, those expectations will frequently contradict one another or meet external opposition; when that happens, the law steps in to slice out a relatively narrow and pragmatic point of policy.[23]

The various treaties differ in many important details but a few guarantees are constant: the rights to life, liberty, equality, due process, and, of course, that which the *Universal Declaration*'s Article 19 describes in deceptively simple terms:

> Everyone has the right to freedom of opinion and expression; this right includes freedom to hold opinions without interference and to seek, receive and impart information and ideas through any media and regardless of frontiers.[24]

"Deceptively" simple? Yes, because the implications, applications, and complications of free expression are nuanced—and because talk isn't always cheap.

When Words Hurt: The Harm Principle

As a teenager, I got a job with an anti-apartheid outfit that involved inviting teenagers from White, Black and Brown segregated schools to get-togethers in church basements. Sometimes, we ranged

---

22 Macklem, *The Sovereignty of Human Rights*, 1.
23 See Frankenberg, 'Human Rights and the Belief in a Just World'.
24 'Universal Declaration of Human Rights' Article 19.

the White children down one wall of the basement, the others opposite, and invited them to describe their daily lives. Most of the White youngsters had never before heard first-hand what it was like to grow up as a second-class citizen under apartheid; most of the others had never before been invited to express what discrimination looked like and felt like. There was yelling; there were tears; there was a lot of silence; later came deeper, quieter talk, and perhaps a hug or two. Many of the young people never met again, but some life-long friendships were formed, some attitudes reshaped, some career paths shifted. In more than a few cases, children went on from these workshops to play leadership roles in bringing down apartheid and in building a democratic society that replaced it.

Speaking and listening helped to change these lives, but freedom of expression was not a "thing" in apartheid South Africa and advocacy for social justice got people into trouble that could include imprisonment, torture, exile, and murder. This has been the way of the world throughout history. When people say unwelcome things, they get told—or forced—to shut up, and some who refuse pay the ultimate price: Socrates, Jesus, Joan of Arc, Gandhi, Martin Luther King, Jr. Over the past two millennia, on all five continents, rulers have come, at varying paces, to allow more people to say more about what they believe until, by the turn of this century, a near-global consensus developed that in democracies, rulers' control over knowledge and power must be limited by other people's freedom to spread information and promote ideas.

But, by that same consensus, the newfound freedom came with limits.

John Stuart Mill, the English liberal whose name is almost synonymous with the modern era's version of free expression, argued that people should be allowed to express "any doctrine, however immoral it may be considered." Even if "all mankind minus one" disagreed with a particular line of thought, people would be "no more justified in silencing that one person than he, if he had the power, would be justified in silencing mankind."[25]

For Mill, arguing against opposing positions was the best way to understand and clarify one's own ideas, and the liberty to make and express free choices was essential to human dignity. Nevertheless, Mill held that all freedom should be subject to what

---

25 Mill, *On Liberty*, chap. II (p. 30).

he (and perhaps only he, ever since) considered a "very simple principle"—that people may exercise power over one another only for the purpose of self-protection or to "prevent harm to others."[26]

Simple or not, Mill's harm principle has proved as resilient as free expression itself. Almost a century after he wrote *On Liberty*, the *European Convention on Human Rights* would guarantee freedom of expression to all, including the right "to receive and impart information and ideas," but subject that freedom to limits including "the interests of national security," prevention of crime, protecting "health or morals" and the reputation of others.[27] A hemisphere away, a scholar of *ubuntu* (a traditionally communitarian ethic amongst Bantu-speaking peoples) provides a fundamentally similar account:

> Freedom of expression is consistent with *ubuntu* as long as the freedoms advocated do not unjustly impinge upon the possibilities and capabilities of others. Stated differently and more broadly, *ubuntu* values freedom that enables oneself and others to be all they can be.[28]

A double-sided democratic consensus appears quite broad, then, that to be free humans, individuals must be granted the right to express their ideas, and that this right should be subject to a general duty to avoid harming other people. But navigating the harm principle requires a moral compass that's calibrated finely enough to answer this question: what kind of potential harm is serious enough to justify depriving people of their right to speak?

The Porous Boundaries of Protected Speech

It's not just in wartime that "loose talk"—thoughtless speech— may cost lives. The most ubiquitously cited example of the harm principle at work is that no one has the right to shout "fire!" in a crowded theatre—unless there really is a fire. In this and many other instances, it's not so much words as their context and purpose that may turn protected speech into a crime; it's usually illegal

---

26 Mill, chap. 1 (page 18).
27 European Convention on Human Rights Article 10(2).
28 Chasi, 'Ubuntu and Freedom of Expression'.

to provoke violence, reveal military secrets, verbally harass people, or threaten them. Damaging a person's reputation is called defamation; lying to cheat someone financially is called fraud. A teacher is contractually expected to follow a school's curriculum, not spend all term talking about their pet peeves. People get thrown out of airports for joking about security measures.

Outside the objective sphere of laws and contracts, calibrating harm gets tougher. During a deadly pandemic outbreak, when lives are saved by clear and consistent public-health education about preventive measures, should scientists be permitted to publicly dispute risks and responses? When should media platforms tolerate or censor offensive opinions about equality, gender, or climate change? Does the harm principle take sides between Palestinians' claims of systemic Israeli oppression and Jews' claims that a secure Israel insures against future genocides?

The most difficult cases arise where a public interest in protecting expression—such as political protests—conflicts with another public interest, such as preventing violence. For people who have lived their lives as objects of others' prejudice, the hearing of hateful messages is a source of pain from which many believe they should be protected. Anti-abortion protestors demand the right to discourage pregnant women from entering an abortion clinic, but those women find it traumatic to face graphic foetal pictures at such a time. If you have donated to a protest movement and that money gets spent on illegal activity, have you facilitated a crime or expressed your political preference?

In these and many other cases, the harm principle fails to resolve disputes because the disagreement lies precisely between competing measurements of harm, leaving some questioning the meaningful existence of a "right" to free expression at all.[29] But as things are in democratic nations those whose public speech is limited and those who apply those limits may see each other in court. That's because, under the rule of law, only the justice system prevents democratic constitutions' being relegated from enforceable expectations to voluntary ethics codes.[30]

---

29 Alexander, *Is There a Right of Freedom of Expression?*, 28.
30 Quinlan, 'The Rule of Law in a Social Media Age', 6–9 (A conscientious reader may expect an echo of this point in later discussion of journalistic standards.).

The benefit of doubt in these disputes will often rest with protecting free expression because this freedom isn't merely a natural implication of individual autonomy. Rather, it provides *everyone* with access to information and ideas of all kinds. As a frequently cited 1997 judgement of the Inter-American Commission on Human Rights expressed it, freedom of expression:

> is indispensable for the formation of public opinion. It is also a *conditio sine qua non* for the development of political parties, trade unions, scientific and cultural societies and, in general, those who wish to influence the public.... Consequently, it can be said that a society that is not well informed is not a society that is truly free.[31]

Still, judges are human, and how they weigh harms and principles will be influenced by their own assumptions as well as the traditions of their legal systems. Some members of an apex court may incline toward interpreting constitutional principles through the moving lens of public attitudes, while others would minimize constitutional barriers to legislatures'—and, therefore, publics'—preferences.[32] Jurisprudence in the United States, for example, has tended to place free expression at the head of a hierarchy of rights, while European courts tend toward seeking equilibrium—for example, citizens' data privacy has been held to outweigh commercial interests in access to information, but not to news organizations' access to, and publication of, information of public interest.[33] Canada's supreme court is somewhere in the middle: it adopts a kind of common-sense case-by-case approach despite that country's constitutional designation of expression, assembly, and belief as "fundamental" freedoms, which some take to imply a degree of precedence.[34] (See Chapter 4.)

Human rights activists often promote a balanced approach rather than a presumption in favour of free expression and other

---

31 Hugo Bustios Saavedra v. Peru, Case 10.548, Report N° 38/97 at 70–71.
32 Binnie and Scalia, 'The Charter at 25 (Debate)'.
33 Petkova, 'Towards an Internal Hierarchy of Values in the EU Legal Order: Balancing the Freedom of Speech and Data Privacy - Bilyana Petkova, 2016'.
34 Cameron, 'Freedom of Expression and the Charter'.

civic rights. As the 1993 World Conference on Human Rights claimed:

> All human rights are universal, indivisible and interdependent and interrelated. The international community must treat human rights globally in a fair and equal manner, on the same footing and with the same emphasis. While the significance of national and regional particularities and various historical, cultural and religious backgrounds must be borne in mind, it is the duty of states, regardless of their political, economic and cultural systems, to promote and protect all human rights and fundamental freedoms.[35]

Whichever approach might be preferred according to a particular country's or group's orientations and traditions, unravelling complex and warring human needs will often resist settling according to a "canned" formula, however lofty its origins. Often, courts will look to one another for guidance, and cite rulings by judges in faraway lands or centuries-old writings by lawyers or philosophers. But when they issue a ruling, it serves as a precedent that guides lower courts for years to come.

If learned judges can disagree about balancing rights, so can other well-meaning people. That's true no matter how high, or low, each disputant ranks speech on their respective, instinctive, hierarchies of rights. Some degree of common sense (and interest-based prejudice!) will be applied by whomever is landed with the unenviable task of settling such disputes. Institutions—schools and universities, hospitals and corporations—will sometimes go this way, sometimes that, in striking a balance, led by their members' and leaders' sense of justice, at best, and crass interests, at worst, within the limits of the law.

It's often unsatisfactory but, in the absence of some (unimaginable) universally accepted unit of measurement for weighing personal harms against broader values, settlement by majority opinion is how justice takes practical form. And at least, with freedom of expression, the citizens, rulers, and laws of democracies all over the world may rely on generally accepted definitions

---

35 Vienna Declaration and Programme of Action, para. 5.

and frameworks through which principles may be litigated into policy.

Much less can be said for freedom of the press—especially in our time.

But, the "Press"?

Many rights charters omit explicit mention of the press, but it's implied by what the *Universal Declaration*'s Article 19 terms the rights "to seek, receive and impart information and ideas through any media." Accordingly, some (but not all) courts have provided journalists with legal privileges such as protecting their sources' identities, gaining access to courts and legislatures, and a degree of leeway when sued for libel.

These and other special protections will be discussed extensively in other chapters. For now, let's merely note the important difference that while freedom of expression is a *general rule* with some exceptions, freedom of the press justifies *exceptions* from selected rules.

The burning questions around freedom of the press in the 2020s include the following. In a world where anyone can, and many do, discover and disseminate information on matters of public interest, what (or who) is the press? Why need the press exist as a distinct entity from direct, unmediated exchanges of knowledge and opinion? Does it merit legal protections? Does it merit public funds and, if so, how can these be reconciled with its demands for autonomy? How have journalists' professional attitudes and ethical assumptions shifted (or not) in response to their desired audiences' changed expectations? How do these trends vary across diverse cultures, information systems, and democratic forms? And what (if any) further alterations are heralded or demanded by emerging consumers and providers of news?

If some of these questions might have seemed rhetorical at the turn of the millennium, today they are all subjects for disputes that expose interlinked knots of assumptions. To begin disentangling these issues, Chapter 2 will pick up the string at its start: the origins of news media, their power and limits, and their core claim of special freedoms.

2 Toward a Free Press

Abstract

This chapter traces the beginnings of journalism—and censorship— from early to modern times in diverse cultural contexts. While freedom of expression includes a universal right to publish in any medium without interference from governments, freedom of the press implies additional protections for news media. Through providing journalists with these privileges, the public asserts its right to receive accurate information on matters of public interest and, especially, to know the truth about how political and economic power is exercised. The disruption of information channels threatens the financial sustainability of news media and challenges journalists' ability to fulfil their functions. A short account of news media's role in the colonial, segregationist, and democratic phases of South African history exemplifies the evolution of press freedom, the unique social role of journalism, and the common limitations of news-media practice.

The Prisoner's Book

"Such is the power of poetry."

With these words, a South African website commemorates the strange origins of the country's national anthem as a composite of two poems written by two men who were both born in 1873 but otherwise could not have had more distinct lives.

The first of these poets, Enoch Sontonga, authored *Nkosi sikelel' i-Afrika* (God Bless Africa), which, after his death, was set to music and became the anthem of anti-*apartheid* resisters.

DOI: 10.4324/9781003223146-2

Sontonga died young in obscurity, but his grave in a "Non-White" cemetery was declared a national monument by Nelson Mandela as president of the newly democratic nation in 1995. Cornelis Jacobus Langenhoven, on the other hand, died revered by Afrikaners as a passionate advocate for their language and culture; his love-poem to the land, *Die Stem* ("the Voice") became the apartheid republic's first and only national song.

Mandela himself is said to have proposed merging the two hymns as just one of his many symbolic acts of reconciliation, and today, the conjoined anthem is belted out by the country's deracialized sports teams and elementary school students alike.

If the power of poetry is one ingredient of this unlikely marriage, it speaks, more broadly, to the power of the written word. For six thousand years or so, people (first in Asia, then everywhere) have been storing information in words for the benefit of people in other places and times. Trillions of words have flowed, for good and ill, on rocks, tablets, scrolls, and pages, in letters and pamphlets and papers and books; factual, fictional, and faked. By the time Nelson Mandela was imprisoned as a revolutionary terrorist—as many journalists "factually" described him during his time—it was easy even for political prisoners to get hold of books.

One such work was a novel about the last days of Jesus Christ, in which a pivotal scene moved Mandela to take an empathic leap from his Robben Island prison cell into the sandals of Pontius Pilate, the Roman governor. Accepting the author's invitation to imagine the trial from Pilate's point of view, Mandela wrote to his wife:

> In that courtroom, authority was not in me as a judge, but was down below in the dock where the prisoner was.[1]

The novel was *Shadows of Nazareth* by the aforementioned Afrikaner poet, C.J. Langenhoven. Years later, the democratically elected President Mandela would explain he'd appreciated both the Afrikaner poet's stylistic light touch and his commitment to cultural transformation. Langenhoven wanted "to free the Afrikaner from the desire to imitate the English," Mandela explained. "His idea was to instil national pride... and so I liked him very much."[2]

---

1 Mandela, *Conversations with Myself*, 274–90.
2 Mandela, 219.

This was an odd thing for a Black liberationist to say of a White man whose "national pride" had led him to co-found the first daily newspaper to publish in Afrikaans. *Die Burger* ("The Citizen") went on to editorially support apartheid with near-religious fidelity; its editors and news angles opposed all progress toward non-racial democracy. It and its sister weekly paper, *Rapport*, were scathing in their criticism of the democratic country's Truth and Reconciliation Commission (TRC), chaired by Archbishop Desmond Tutu in the 1990s: editorials described it as a witch-hunt against Afrikaners and dubbed it *"Tutu se bieg en liegkommissie"* (a rhyming jab meaning, "Tutu's commission of confessions and lies").[3]

More than a hundred Afrikaner journalists themselves later made submissions to the TRC, acknowledging that they had collectively helped to create a political climate that made human-rights abuses possible, and had believed the White government's claims too readily. Yet, after Mandela's transition from prisoner to president, those same journalists kept their readers informed about the vital changes going on in their country—including the seven-years-long proceedings of the TRC. As one Afrikaner journalist wrote during the commission's early years:

> Had it not been for the TRC, many Afrikaners (and other White South Africans) would never have... heard a victim of apartheid telling his or her story. Afrikaners and some of their newspapers may not have liked the TRC but, like it or not, reporters at these papers told them the stories and many of their readers read them. What this means is that... few in South Africa can truthfully say: I did not know.[4]

Such is the power of the press.

Birth of a Liberty

When constitutional lawyers refer to the press, they generally mean what people often call "the media" these days. Both terms are confusing. Printing presses, broadcast channels and digital media all produce varied kinds of entertaining stuff that has nothing to do

---

3 Du Plessis, 'Newspaper Management Keeps Quiet...'
4 Du Plessis.

with news and to which discussions about freedom are mostly irrelevant. But in the narrower sense (which is generally applied in this book), the press consists of the people who use any and all media forms to provide information about current events—that is, news.

News is much older than platforms, presses, and journalism. When the first messenger returned to their native village to tell of a hunted animal slain or tribal battle won, that report of recent events marked the birth of news. Visual media followed in the symbolic rock art of San people in southern Africa, perhaps seventy thousand years ago,[5] and precursors of networked journalism have been hypothesized in the Indigenous communication networks of the Americas.[6] Ancient couriers were occasionally killed for bearing unwelcome tidings, as with the unfortunate Amalekite who told the Israelite king David of a battle lost and was killed for his trouble,[7] but it is more often considered unlawful, impious, or unwise to punish those who faithfully—and truthfully—carry unwelcome messages.[8]

Perhaps it's no great stretch to find in this ethos of protecting messengers the earliest seed of freedom of the press, long before presses themselves were invented in the stamps of east Asia. While monks in medieval Europe were using quills to copy scrolls one at a time, people in Hangzhou, capital of the Southern Song dynasty, sold and bought unofficial periodicals containing both news and commentary known as the *xiao-pao* ("illegal paper"). According to Yangming He's analysis of classical Chinese literature, these earliest newspapers-of-sorts were produced by:

> ...some staff of the information department [who] privately worked with civilians—non-government employees—to compile information that failed to meet the editing deadline or failed to obtain permission to be disclosed to the public.[9]

About two centuries later, when darkness began lifting over feudal Europe, something resembling news was carried from court to

---

5 Miyagawa, Lesure, and Nóbrega, 'Cross-Modality Information Transfer'.
6 Conboy, 'Journalism History', 26.
7 Galpaz-Feller, 'David and the Messenger'.
8 Wilson-Lee, 'Killing the Messenger', 583–84.
9 Yangming He, 'Hangzhou, the Origins of the World Press and Journalism?'

court by troubadours or *meistersingers*. One Michael Beheim won fame in the fifteenth century for rhymed reports including the feature profile (as we might say today) of a bloodthirsty Wallachian prince who was said to partake of human blood. As media historians Brian Winston and Matthew Winston argue, the tale of Prince Tracul is one of many manifestations of pre-Twitter news distortion:

> Beheim is but a step away from fictional imagining, his mainstream news story being not totally mendacious, but certainly significantly distorted. The roots of fake news in the mainstream media are all to be found in this contemporary account of the historical figure who would become the fictional "Dracula"— not a lie but, at best, a necessarily partial truth.[10]

A breakthrough came that same century when someone figured out how to print hundreds of pages a minute, which was much faster than one-page-at-a-time Chinese and Indian presses and faster even than some home-office printers in use today. That someone was probably not the Rhineland's Johann Gutenberg, but it was he who invented moveable type, which made multi-page productions (such as books) feasible.[11]

And so, finally, was born the age of mass media, in which people living in different places could receive identical pieces of information all produced, within the same eye-blink, somewhere else altogether. The early media products covered a spectrum of purpose and subject matter including art, faith, entertainment, and, yes, news. First came single-topic "newsbooks" and one-off general-update broadsheet "bills of news," and then in Strasbourg around 1605, the first periodicals close in purpose to a newspaper. Dutch equivalents followed, and then English and French translations distributed from Amsterdam.[12]

It took until the late 1700s for kings, lords, and bishops to start worrying. Newspapers had added editorial opinion columns to staples such as reports on sex scandals, advertisements, cartoons,

---

10 Winston and Winston, *The Roots of Fake News*, 19.
11 Barbier, *Gutenberg's Europe*.
12 Anderson, Downie, and Schudson, *The News Media*, 20.

puzzles, and advice columns.[13] Rulers accustomed to deciding what people should know and think about current events saw the new platforms as "socially and politically disruptive."[14] Few commoners could read, but those who could possessed lips, and the rest had ears.

And so to censorship.

As rulers imposed their will on the disruptive new technology, printers used it to promote a brand-new idea: freedom to publish. During the eighteenth-century reign of England's King George III, someone pen-named Junius wrote several essays that denounced arbitrary power and affirmed what was necessary to counter it:

> Let it be impressed upon your minds, let it be instilled into your children, that the liberty of the press is the *palladium* of all the civil, political, and religious rights of an Englishman.[15]

Three of Junius's brave publishers were prosecuted for seditious libel (treasonous defamation of officials); one of these trials ended in conviction, one in acquittal, and one in a dauntless jury returning the impressively imaginative verdict of, "Guilty of printing and publishing only."[16] Faced with rising liberal advocacy, several European rulers now pulled back on censorship; the king of Sweden was first to proclaim freedom of the press into law, in 1766,[17] followed by post-revolutionary regimes in and beyond Europe.[18] But the extent of printers' liberty continued to be litigated.

From Debut to Disruption (A View from South Africa)

The past two centuries of journalism in South Africa provide a handy canvass on which to sketch paradigmatic steps in the evolution of press freedom. From its European colonial origins, *via* a fiery adolescence under tyranny's thumb, to the challenges of

---

13 Winston and Winston, *The Roots of Fake News*, 45.
14 Conboy, 'Journalism History', 28.
15 Anonymous, *The Letters of Junius* (i).
16 Stephen, 'Chatham, Francis, and Junius', 239.
17 Skuncke, 'Freedom of the Press and Social Equality in Sweden, 1766–1772'.
18 Martin, 'From the "free and Open" Press to the "Press of Freedom"'.

young adulthood in contemporary Africa, the press has made halting progress toward enjoying liberty and proving worthy of it. Each of those three developmental stages of South African journalism mirrors a key step in the evolution of a free press.

The journey starts in the Cape Colony in January, 1824.

Birth of an African Press

It took only a few weeks of publication for Africa's first independent newspaper to incur the wrath of government.[19] A printer from London named George Greig founded the *South African Commercial Advertiser* against the asserted will of the British governor of the Cape Colony. What happened next was described decades later by one of Greig's printing apprentices in a memoir (on which the following summary largely relies) whose epigraph reads: "The mass of every people must be barbarous where there is no printing."[20]

British law gave the governor, Lord Charles Somerset, no say over a newspaper's right to exist, but he could and did impose a levy on the *Advertiser*. This state of grace lasted only until the paper started running news reports from a court case brought by a government official for libel. This was "straight news," devoid of commentary, written in the plain, almost stenographic style that still characterizes daily court reporting in many of the world's publications.

As reported by the paper, the colony's tax collector had been accused, in a letter of complaint addressed to officials in England, of trafficking "Prize Negroes" (indentured former slaves) for financial gain and personal favours. The letter had been intercepted before leaving the Cape, and the outraged tax collector brought charges against the whistle-blower for "seditious libel," a criminal offence. Now, thanks to the *Advertiser*'s reporting, every literate colonist could read every detail of the allegations. If this intrusion

---

19 Africa's "first newspaper" is sometimes given as *Annonces, affiches et avis divers pour les colonies des isles de France et de Bourbon*, in Mauritius, but that was a government publication, as was a similar periodical of government notices in the Cape.
20 Meurant, *Sixty Years Ago*.

was not unsettling enough to the Cape's tiny ruling elite, still more insolent was the editorial comment that followed the letter-writer's acquittal. Outraged, Governor Somerset ordered that future proofs of the *Advertiser* be submitted for approval before publication.

Greig refused, preferring to suspend production of his paper. He also distributed a free one-off sheet called "The Facts," which described blow by blow how the governor's censorship had been carried out. Somerset then confiscated Greig's printing equipment, and Greig was on the next ship to London, where he took his case to the Lords of the Treasury. His plea was both simple and successful: the British regime of press freedom should apply in equal measure to the Crown's colonies.

By the time the vindicated publisher had returned to the Cape to reclaim his equipment and restart his paper, Lord Charles was himself on a boat home, for good. As with Junius's printers, so also with the *Advertiser* and parallel battles that publishers (not journalists) fought one by one in those early days, press freedom advanced mainly through someone trying to shoot it down, and the target demanding justice.

Equally significant was the cause of the Greig-Somerset shoot-out. The paper's offence was to disseminate accurate news about a public official's alleged corruption. This was work that lay close to the core function on which the first arguments for press freedom had rested: to provide accurate information about public affairs. The implications of these conjoined, co-dependent ideas—the *rights* and the *purposes* of news media—will be a developing theme of this book's argument.

The Apartheid Years

The next epoch of South African history—and of journalism's evolution—began in 1948 with the election of an Afrikaner-led, determinedly segregationist government. The National Party's legislation replaced the mannered British approach to enforcing White privilege with gunpoint deportations to impoverished rural "homelands" and restrictions on movement that underpinned apartheid. All children would now attend separate schools, interracial marriage was made illegal, and the number of Black and Brown people voting in parliamentary elections declined from a privileged few to zero. Enforcing these and other measures required an array of laws that were brutally policed.[21]

If the tyranny was often ignored or explained away by Afrikaans-language press, the English papers covered what they noticed while obeying to the letter an array of laws that inhibited reporting on political and security matters. Outside the main media groups, alternative papers pushed the legal envelope more forthrightly. The lowest point of press freedom was reached in 1977, when the government banned the largest newspaper serving Black audiences, *The World*, and security police detained and interrogated its editor, Percy Qoboza, for five months, before releasing him without charge or trial.[22]

Some portrayals of the press in those cruel decades focus on journalists' collaborative relaying of the racist system's lies; the Truth and Reconciliation Commission found that most news publications had either expressly promoted apartheid, or implicitly complied with it.[23] Other accounts spotlight the many intrepid reporters who faced down police and the editors who insisted on digging out unsavoury truths.[24] I was a journalist in South Africa in the 1970s and early 1980s, including periods reporting for European newspapers and editing a monthly church newspaper with a focus on social justice. Here, for what it's worth, is my recollection of what journalists did: we brought our backgrounds, biases, aspirations, vulnerabilities, and various mixes of courage and cowardice to work every day. We earned alternating degrees of admiration, anonymity, and shame.

And, despite the many failings of our work, facts got out.

Both sides of this equation have significance to a global understanding of press freedom. That journalists bring capacities for both accomplishment and failure to their work should not get forgotten in later chapters, which address questions of

---

21 Except where otherwise cited, information about political and journalistic developments in this chapter is drawn from in-person and telephone interviews conducted with Stefaans Brümmer, Anton Harber, and others in February and March 2022 and subsequent email correspondence, and on the author's personal experience.
22 'Black Wednesday, the Banning of 19 Black Consciousness Movement Organisations'.
23 Berger, 'Problematizing Race for Journalists'.
24 Harber, *Southern African Muckraking*.

truthfulness, of privileges, and of accountability. If journalism is worth fostering, it's not because journalists are considered virtuous but because their purpose and routines are considered useful. People's arguments about press freedom are sometimes distractingly posited on idealism, but a cool stock-taking of realities is more helpful when discussing matters of social policy.

The Democratic Reckoning

The third and current era of press and politics in South Africa began with the election of Nelson Mandela as president in 1994 and the adoption, soon afterward, of a new constitution that included this guarantee:

Everyone has the right to freedom of expression, which includes

a. freedom of the press and other media;
b. freedom to receive or impart information or ideas;
c. freedom of artistic creativity; and
d. academic freedom and freedom of scientific research.

Excluded from this right were "war propaganda," incitement to violence, and "advocacy of hatred that is based on race, ethnicity, gender or religion, and that constitutes incitement to cause harm."[25]

Around this time, a young journalist named Stefaans Brümmer was gaining attention as a rookie reporter who would go the distance to dig out an important story. Assigned to the supposedly prosaic shipping beat at a Cape Town daily, *The Argus*, young Brümmer had covered a missing sailor, fires both at sea and in the harbour, and an Antarctic rescue. He hopped a ship carrying relief to victims of the war in Somalia and stayed a while to report on the war itself. Back home, he covered the 1992 Bhisho Massacre, in which police shot and killed an estimated twenty-eight anti-segregation protesters.[26] A few years later, he was hired by the storied investigative unit of the *Mail & Guardian* in Johannesburg.

---

25 'Constitution of the Republic of South Africa', sec. 16.
26 'Bhisho Massacre Memorial This Thursday'.

Brümmer had developed a passion for investigative reporting—the kind that exposes secret wrongdoing. He calls this work "digging for dung" (a peculiarly African version of "muckraking") and today admits to having become fixated on it:

> There's something about exposing... truths that the masses would hopefully find useful to improve the condition of society. And once you think of things in that way, and I think most investigative journalists do, then how do you not become a bit obsessive about it?[27]

When democracy dawned, more swiftly than any journalists (or almost anyone else) had predicted, the *Mail & Guardian* kept on trucking; the way its editors saw it, the change of government meant a new group of power-holders on whom journalists must keep watch. But the legacy of racist rule did not lend itself to a clean reboot of relationships between the press, still largely owned by Whites, and the newly empowered former revolutionaries. A turn-of-the-millennium investigation by the South African Human Rights Commission reported a "remarkable consensus" among witnesses that newsrooms were still pervaded by systemic and subliminal discrimination and a tendency to deny racism's existence. "South African media can be characterised as racist institutions," it concluded. "This finding holds regardless as to whether there is conscious or unconscious racism, direct or indirect."[28]

Tension between the press and leaders of the ruling African National Congress (ANC) would be fuelled over the coming years by investigative teams' cumulative exposure of government corruption. And right then, as the millennium turned, came another, more global, revolution—the maturing of the social web and resulting global economic challenges to news-media businesses everywhere.

Investigative journalism is expensive almost by definition: it takes months of reporting time to dig up and verify secrets of public importance. When news organizations get those facts

---

27 de Villiers, 'Stefaans Brümmer, AmaBhungane Co-Founder, on Crooks, Graft and Why He's Moving on'.
28 Pityana et al., 'Faultlines: Inquiry into Racism in the Media', 89.

wrong, they risk potentially ruinous lawsuits for libel, so their budgets must include high legal costs. By 2009 (five years after the birth of Facebook spurred the launches of successive social media platforms), it had become clear that the *Mail & Guardian*, like newspapers around the world, was no longer earning enough advertising and subscription revenue to cover its commitment to major investigative reports.

Brümmer huddled with a colleague and they came up with a new idea that they somehow sold to the paper's owners: the three-person investigative unit would leave the payroll and become an independent non-profit. It would train a new generation of young journalists with philanthropic support, and provide all its reports to the *Mail & Guardian* in exchange for fees totalling the unit's existing budget.

It was a good deal for all, and the investigative project was launched under the name, *amaBhungane*, which is Zulu for "the dung beetles."[29] Its first outside help came in the form of a one-million-rand annual grant (then worth about seventy thousand euros) from the Open Society philanthropic collective founded by George Soros. While the exclusive arrangement with the *Mail & Guardian* ended seven years later, *amaBhungane* continues, at time of writing, to be the country's leading source of anticorruption investigations. The team led the charge in exposing so-called "state capture" by associates of then-president Jacob Zuma in the mid-2010s, joined by the entrepreneurially owned *Daily Maverick* web-focused operation and *News24*, a division of the massive media company that grew out of Langenhoven's *Die Burger*.[30]

Such, one might say, is the power of a free press. And indeed, at time of writing three decades into the democratic era, the country still enjoys relatively high international scores for press freedom. On the Reporters Without Borders (RSF) index, it stands about half way between the Netherlands and Australia and is described as enjoying a "sturdy, diverse and dynamic" media landscape marred by a "resurgence of verbal and physical attacks against journalists by political activists."[31] The Reuters Institute measured

29 *Author's Disclosure*: I have occasionally served as a voluntary writing coach for *amaBhungane*'s young journalists.
30 Harber, *So, for the Record*; Wasserman, 'The State of South African Media'.
31 'RSF's 2022 World Press Freedom Index'.

South African trust in media as second only to Finland's among surveyed countries in 2022.[32]

Investigative journalism on matters of public interest certainly continues to thrive, with *amaBhungane* only one of several major contributors to the field. One of the country's great advocates for quality journalism, former *Mail & Guardian* editor Anton Harber, told me he sometimes worries about the proportion of work that "feeds off corruption," rather than looking into development, policy achievements, and options for tackling challenges such as employment, housing, and energy. Journalists' credibility took a major knock when the *Sunday Times*, the country's biggest paper, retracted and apologized for a series of stories that wrongly accused innocent people of corruption.[33] The subsequent report of an inquiry commissioned for the national editors' forum found "systemic problems imperilling ethical conduct across the whole media landscape" including:

> revenue challenges impacting on sustainability; the related diminution of resources for professional development and training and for the effective exercise of editorial and sub-editing checks and balances; the social media-fuelled pressure to break stories ever faster amidst competing mis- and disinformation narratives; societal pressures—including harassment and official disdain and manipulation—on reporters; and lacunae in the scope and powers of regulatory bodies.[34]

Among these challenges, none is unique to South Africa and most lie close to the core of what's meant by news-media disruption. This idea applies an economic theory, developed in the 1990s by Clayton Christensen of Harvard Business School, that describes how innovators erode established industries through finding new, more effective and less costly ways to "do the job" that customers require. In the case of digital information, nimble tech-savvy newcomers embraced and adapted web-based infrastructures to deliver information much faster and more efficiently than was possible for the analogue press barons of the twentieth

---

32 Newman et al., 'Digital News Report 2021', 158.
33 Harber, 'How to Ensure Media Is Not a Pawn for Politicians'.
34 Satchwell, Bikitsha, and Mkhondo, 'Independent Panel Report', 1.

century. Questioning all traditional approaches and constraints, the innovators "created new market demand by engaging new audiences" (in the words of Christensen and David Skok) with novel and personalized content.[35]

As disruption shook news businesses, almost all conventional wisdom seemed up for grabs including what journalists do and how and why they do it. One idea, however, remained deeply embedded and has, indeed, gone unquestioned so far in these pages, including the above visits to epochs in South African journalism. It's the assumption that journalism's enduring "job," and therefore social value, has something to do with monitoring governments, institutions, and potentates.

Particular Roles, Particular Rights

Where news media win legal privileges or public support under the heading of press freedom, their claim rests on the importance of letting people know what's happening in their communities, nations, and world. In this view, independent news media are necessary to expose corruption and abuse of power through providing truthful information including "all possible views" that bear on the decisions that a democracy's citizens make.[36]

The most basic liberty implied by this role of the press was also the first to be won: freedom from censorship. William Blackstone's influential four-volume Commentaries on the Laws of England (published 1765–1769) asserted that "liberty of the press is indeed essential to the nature of a free state," but immediately qualified this liberty's scope. It provided, not a get-out-of-jail-free entitlement for publishers, but a guarantee only against "prior restraints" on publication:

> Every freeman has an undoubted right to lay what sentiments he pleases before the public: to forbid this, is to destroy the freedom of the press: but if he publishes what is improper, mischievous, or illegal, he must take the consequence of his own temerity.[37]

---

35 Christensen, Skok, and Allworth, 'Breaking News'.
36 Nimmer, 'Introduction--Is Freedom of the Press a Redundancy', 653.
37 Per Bird, *The Revolution in Freedoms of Press and Speech*, 21.

Blackstone seems to have ignored more ambitious affirmations in the jurisprudence of his time, such as the right to publicly—and truthfully—criticize "the pernicious tendency of public measures."[38] But most democracies have, in the centuries since, renovated the modest shelter in which Blackstone accommodated press freedom. The twentieth century's broad constitutional protections went well beyond mere freedom from censorship—a freedom meant to be enjoyed by everyone—to something extra, specific to "the press."

An "Enabling Environment" for Newsgathering

A broad swath of constitutional jurisprudence requires news-media liberty to be manifested long before censors have something to censor. As defined by Reporters Without Borders (RSF), press freedom means:

> ...the effective possibility for journalists, as individuals and as groups, to select, produce and disseminate news and information in the public interest, independently from political, economic, legal and social interference, and without threats to their physical and mental safety.[39]

Viewed robustly, press freedom thus covers not just the production of news but everything involved in newsgathering. The right to "seek, receive and impart" facts and opinions is theoretically guaranteed as a condition of United Nations membership,[40] but the rules for doing so, contained in the International Covenant on Civil and Political Rights, include much fine print. Exercising free expression "carries special duties and responsibilities," the treaty states, and may therefore be restricted by law to respect "the rights or reputations of others" and to protect national security, public order, or "public health or morals."[41]

That's a significant amount of wiggle room, but, in fairness, it's just a fact of life that values—including the wide range of

---

38 Bird, 25.
39 'RSF's 2022 World Press Freedom Index'.
40 'Universal Declaration of Human Rights', art. 19.
41 'International Covenant on Civil and Political Rights', art. 19.

proclaimed freedoms—must sometimes be weighed against one another, whether on the grand scale of international politics or in the ethics of ordinary life. In a matter of medical emergency, for instance, a patient's right to privacy may be thought secondary to their right to life.

A common tool for balancing legal rights is to place them in categories that allow for broad distinctions of purpose and measures of necessity. One example is the distinction between civil and natural rights. Natural rights allow people to live in safety, equality, and dignity, and many think they trump other, more complex, kinds of freedom. On the other hand, the civil rights to vote, to strike, and—yes—to be heard on matters of public policy, may be the best way to protect natural rights. So, the difference between natural and civil rights doesn't necessarily mean one should override the other.

In fact, a fair (but not perfect) consensus has emerged over the centuries that some civil rights belong, along with natural rights, in a "core" of fundamental rights. Both equality rights and the prohibition of slavery obviously are fundamental because they have clear value in themselves. Why should no one be tortured, or arbitrarily detained? Because no one should be treated that way—period.[42] Why should people be treated equally? Because the designers of constitutions hold such "truths," in Abraham Lincoln's words, "to be self-evident."

An Instrumental Right

The freedom to voice one's ideas is often considered fundamental for democratic society or even—as argued by Zac Gershberg and Sean Illing—the *single* defining feature of democracy, from which other good things (such as equality before the law) might flow.[43] This is why anyone—not just the editor of *Die Welt* but a small-town blogger in the Bavarian Alps—has an equal claim against censorship.

By contrast, instrumental rights are needed, not because they are good in themselves, but in order to foster the fundamental freedoms. Freedom of the press is one such right, required, in

---

42 Koji, 'Emerging Hierarchy in International Human Rights and Beyond', 927.
43 Gershberg and Illing, *The Paradox of Democracy*, 41.

Junius's own words, to protect "all the civil, political, and religious rights" of society at large.[44]

It's not journalists who need, for instance, to protect a confidential source; rather, the public needs information that's sometimes obtained confidentially. This is the form of argument on which relevant UNESCO documents have expanded since the Windhoek Declaration of 1991.[45] According to this framework, news media freedom implies more than the mere absence of "control, censorship, or harassment" by the state; it also requires several vital protections, sometimes called "positive rights," which comprise an "enabling environment" including:

> ...access to information guarantees, civil defamation laws based on international standards, and protections for the confidentiality of journalist sources and whistle-blowers, among other legal and statutory preconditions....
>
> For full press freedom, these components that shape the character of media freedom need themselves to be accompanied by pluralism and independence...[which] are also dramatically affected by the rise of internet gatekeepers, the eroding business model for journalism, and the levels of competence of news media audiences to engage with communications.[46]

These claims of particular rights rest on journalism's particular role—that of providing accurate information on public affairs. But, as Chapter 3 will show, disruption has challenged the very foundations of that argument. Freedom, it turns out, comes at a price.

---

44 Anonymous, *The Letters of Junius* (i).
45 'Declaration of Windhoek'.
46 Benequista, *Journalism Is a Public Good*, 45.

3 The End of The Press That Was

Abstract

This chapter shows how digital disruption and resultant "information disorder" pose powerful challenges to freedom of the press. Well beyond the mere absence of censorship, news media have won a range of instrumentally justified legal privileges or exemptions. Examples of these so-called positive rights include protection of confidential sources' identities, preferred access to spaces and documents, limits to the inhibitory force of privacy and defamation laws, and—increasingly in recent years—various kinds of financial relief. As recent Canadian examples demonstrate, news media disruption has made it difficult to distinguish journalists from other potential claimants to press privileges without limiting the public's right to choose amongst plural and diverse sources of fact and opinion—another vital indicator of press freedom. The competing claimants include smaller or more peripheral providers of news, campaigners for causes of various kinds, and the purveyors of disinformation. As well, the harm done by online disinformation and hate has bolstered moves toward enforced moderation of online content.

"Good Faith:" The Policing of a Journalist's Mind

On Friday, November 20, 2021, on a forest road in north-western Canada, 15 people were arrested at a blockade erected by members of the Wet'suwet'en Indigenous nation. They were there to protest a gas company's pipeline development on their traditional land. The blockade was illegal, and a court had ordered the area cleared.

DOI: 10.4324/9781003223146-3

One of those detained by federal police was a 37-year-old woman who had been photographing the protest. Her name: Amber Bracken. Her profession: photojournalist. Her assignment: covering the protest for *The Narwhal*, an investigative magazine focused on environmental issues.[1] Bracken kept shooting photos while under arrest, a reaction she later attributed less to courage than to reflex:

> My knees and all my joints were totally trembling. And I remember thinking I wasn't sure if I was safe to move my hands because the ... people I was photographing had their hands in the air.... I look now at some of the pictures I did do in there, and I think I could have done better.[2]

Journalists and press-freedom advocates from Canada condemned the arrests of Bracken and a documentary producer, Michael Toledano, who was filming the Wet'suwet'en blockade. Bracken herself later commented that the experience left her "very frustrated" at the state of press freedom in Canada.[3]

By then, Bracken was already one of her country's most celebrated photojournalists, with work published in leading international news titles and winning multiple awards. Her accolades would soon include the 2022 World Press Photo of the Year, for a haunting twilight photo for *The New York Times* of an impromptu memorial for Indigenous children who died in residential schools.[4]

But Bracken's arrest at the Wet'suwet'en pipeline blockade was no mere mistake. Both she and Toledano had identified themselves as journalists, but a police superintendent, commenting later, questioned their motives—whether they were at the scene to support the protests or to conduct newsgathering in "good faith."

This was an implicit reference to an appeal court judgement in another province about whether journalists are covered by

---

1 Partridge, 'Wet'suwet'en Camp Leader, Journalists Arrested'.
2 Lederman, 'Canadian Amber Bracken Wins World Press Photo of the Year for Residential School Memorial Photo'; Jacobsen, 'Opinion'.
3 Lederman, 'Canadian Amber Bracken Wins World Press Photo of the Year for Residential School Memorial Photo'; Jacobsen, 'Opinion'; 'Canadian Charter of Rights and Freedoms', para. 2(b).
4 Bracken, 'Kamloops Residential School'.

injunctions against protests. That court had advised consideration of whether the person claiming exemption is "engaged in apparent good faith in a news-gathering activity of a journalistic nature" on a matter of public interest or, conversely, aiding protesters or interfering with law enforcement.[5]

Bracken herself had made no pretence of neutrality regarding the issues at stake in the blockade. She has described her interest as lying at the "intersection of photography, journalism and public service" with a focus on Indigenous people's empowerment and struggle for justice. In her work, she seeks "to represent and foster that strength while documenting issues around culture, environment and the effects of intergenerational trauma from colonization."[6]

Because the pipeline company withdrew its civil contempt complaint a few weeks after the arrests, the charges against Bracken were dropped without hearing arguments on her status at the blockade: was she there as a journalist on the job or as a "participant" in an illegal gathering?

It seems that the police in this case deemed at least part of the answer to reside in Bracken's mind. They considered her presence at the blockade to be an expression of sympathy for the protestors' cause, a kind of "advocacy" or "assistance," rather than newsgathering in "good faith."[7] By the latter, they seemed to mean something like a neutral approach to recording of events. From that point of view, even the circulation of sympathetic images could be viewed as "participation" in a cause.

At issue in this case and many others like it is something bigger than a difference of perspective between a police officer and an arrestee: it's a tricky question about the relationship between journalists' rights and journalism's purposes. How we understand that relationship begins to define what press freedom offers in the way of protections and privileges, who may claim them, and under what conditions and circumstances.

These questions may have seemed of mostly academic interest until the current age of news-media disruption; now, they're impossible to avoid.

---

5 'Coastal GasLink Drops Charges'; Re Brake; Anderson v. Nalcor Energy, 2019 NLCA at 84.
6 Bracken, 'About Me'.
7 'Coastal GasLink Drops Charges'.

Rights Reserved, with Conditions Attached

Canada's constitutional Charter of Rights and Freedoms includes a guarantee of "freedom of thought, belief, opinion and expression, including freedom of the press and other media of communication."[8] The idea of "including" press or media freedom under the heading of expression is not unusual in constitutional law and reflects an obvious truth: publishing is a way of speaking. But, as noted above, journalism's unique role starts well before anything gets published; what earns special protections is *gathering* information of public interest.

This difference is important, because freedom of expression is mostly protected by negative rights—that is, the *absence* of hindrances such as censorship. Newsgathering, on the other hand, involves positive claims, two of which have been mentioned in previous chapters—protection of confidential sources and access to restricted spaces.

Positive and negative claims impose different types of obligation on others.[9] Let's say you and I are strolling by a torrential river, discussing press freedom; you are using a sturdy branch as a walking stick. Swept away by the force of my argument, I lose my footing, tumble, and suddenly face getting swept away altogether. So here's the question: what do you with your stick? If my right to life is a purely negative claim, you should keep it away from my head. If my claim is positive, you stick it where my hands are going.

A libertarian approach to human rights stops at the overarching negative right to live autonomously, which is why Frédéric Bastiat, writing in 1850, famously refuted fraternity as a right: it necessarily impedes on liberty, in his view.[10] But the liberal view, which underpins human-rights law, requires that governments protect both negative and positive rights.

---

8 'Canadian Charter of Rights and Freedoms', sec. 2(b).
9 Normative distinctions between positive and negative claims, rights, claims, or freedoms are similar in formulation, but not in purpose, to the philosophical notion of positive and negative types of self-actualizing "liberty," as prominently explored by Isaiah Berlin. See Berlin, 'Two Concepts of Liberty'.
10 Bastiat, 'The Law (Chapter 2)'.

Newsgathering: A Contingent Freedom

Because the public has a right to know what's going on, journalists get to do some things that others can't. Consider, for example, the "press gallery." In legislatures across the globe, reporters get the best seat in the house, plus a ticket to meet with legislators in spaces where ordinary citizens just can't go. That's not because legislators enjoy reporters' company. In the words of a United Kingdom parliamentary clerk in 1964: "The press are here on sufferance." The earliest printed accounts of proceedings in Westminster's "mother of parliaments" were burned or censored, a step forward from amputating the hands of early adopters of shorthand who transcribed public speeches in the Roman Empire and medieval Europe.[11] But eighteenth-century reporters persevered, and eventually their parliamentary news stories were ripped from the headlines by a printer named John Hansard and published as the closest approximation of an official record.[12] Without the quill-scribblings of those early journalists, legislatures might have remained, for practical purposes, as secluded a space as the king's privy-council chambers.

Today, the holder of a press pass may gain access to a parliamentary lobby or to the nether regions of a sports arena. Of course, if *everyone* had press badges, no one would wear them. The rights they provide are not attached to the chronic condition of being human but reserved to the acute condition of being a journalist, and reserved rights usually come with conditions attached. Because these reserved rights are justified by what the public (rather than the journalist) needs, they extend no further than the purpose of serving the public interest.[13] Permission to take a camera into the athletes' changing area may stop where the showers start; a parliamentary pass fosters the asking of questions about politicians' intentions but not about their sex lives. As a precedent-setting decision of South Africa's constitutional court put it in 2002:

---

11 Vice and Farrell, 'The History of Hansard', 2.
12 Vice and Farrell, 2–7.
13 Lichtenberg, 'Foundations and Limits of Freedom of the Press'.

Every citizen has the right to freedom of the press and the media and the right to receive information and ideas. ... The ability of each citizen to be a responsible and effective member of our society depends upon the manner in which the media carry out their constitutional mandate. The media thus rely on freedom of expression and must foster it. In this sense they are both bearers of rights and bearers of constitutional obligations in relation to freedom of expression.[14]

To clarify this point, let's examine a different, yet also oft-disputed, matter: the reserved right of police officers to shoot people.

Policing has been deemed necessary in most places in order to safeguard the general population's rights (universal human rights!) to life, security, free movement, and more. But doing this work effectively means confronting armed and violent criminals. Therefore, police may be allowed to use weapons in ways prohibited to others. This right is not a fundamental entitlement of being human; it is justified only instrumentally—to protect a necessary function (policing). Therefore, this particular right is contingent on police officers' doing the work that society expects of them. Ergo, police have no right to shoot just because they don't, say, like the colour of someone's skin.

Put more concisely, the particular rights reserved for police come glued to a particular obligation: "to serve and protect." When the obligation takes second place to the right, people start calling for police departments to be defunded.

Similarly, because the work of journalistic newsgathering has been deemed necessary to foster the public's need for factual information, newsgatherers claim particular rights that are, again, contingent on their particular purpose. Ergo, a parliamentary journalist selling subscriptions to their blog in the members' lounge could be asked to leave.

Other common press entitlements include allowing journalists to protect their sources by claiming exemption from search warrants and subpoenas,[15] to see court documents in real time, and to communicate with the outside world during trials even where that's normally prohibited. In some jurisdictions, journalists are allowed

---

14 Khumalo and Others v Holomisa, 2002 (5) SA 401 (CC) at 22.
15 Ichou, *World Trends in Freedom of Expression and Media Development*, 81ff.

to attend hearings that are closed to the public;[16] in the United Kingdom, reporting is now allowed in some family courts.[17]

The list of entitlements goes on. To limit the risks of exposing wrongdoing, many countries' defamation laws protect journalists who take demonstrably fair and responsible steps to get at the truth.[18] (More on this in Chapter 5.) Some jurisdictions exempt news media from data privacy laws,[19] search-and-seizure rules,[20] and other, occasionally esoteric affordances: the Canadian province of Ontario exempts undercover journalists from prosecutions for trespass in food-chain facilities.[21]

These are just some examples of positive rights implied by the freedom of the press. As the rest of this chapter will show, disruption has both expanded the list and complicated the question of who may claim them.

Privileging a "Qualified" Press (A View from Canada)

"*Je ne réponds pas aux questions des* Rebel News."

Nine words are unusually few for a politician's comment at a nationally televised news conference, and when they translate to a point-blank refusal to answer questions from a news publication, one might suspect iron-man bluster. But in this case, the brush-off was the first of several by party leaders in Canada's federal election of 2021, including the prime minister, in scrums following the party leaders' official debate in Ottawa.[22] The only surprise was that the scrums included envoys from *Rebel News* at all.

Rebel News, a right-wing alternative web-based publication, had consistently been denied access to federal and provincial legislatures' press galleries.[23] But here it was, thanks to successful court appeals against official refusals of its accreditation during two successive federal elections.

---

16 Johnston and Wallace, 'Who Is a Journalist? Changing Legal Definitions in a de-Territorialised Media Space'.
17 Granger, 'New Powers for UK Media to Report on Family Courts'.
18 Barendt, 'Reynolds Revived and Replaced'.
19 Korpisaari, 'The Journalistic Exemption in Personal Data Processing'.
20 Cameron, 'Section 2(b)'s Other Fundamental Freedom'.
21 General Regulation under the Security from Trespass and Protecting Food Security Act, S.O. 2020, c.9.
22 *Canada Election 2021* from 2:52:00.
23 Boyd, 'Accreditation and Access in a Changing Media Landscape'.

The publication's claim to be a news platform was controversial. The brand's stated mission was to provide alternatives to "mainstream media" narratives—"a side of the story you won't get anywhere else"—but critics called it a far-right purveyor of fake news. On a randomly selected day in September, 2022, its home page featured stories about "climate lockdowns," a cancelled comedian, and the launch of a documentary purporting to expose "the buried truth" about unmarked graves at residential schools for Indigenous children. Also, the birth of a fringe provincial party opposed to digital identification cards, sex-change treatments for children, and "progressive gender-based ideologies fed to youth."[24] Since-deleted content has included a 2016 interview with an Austrian neo-Nazi about "Europe's disastrous immigration policies" and articles about "white genocide" and "population replacement" in Canada.[25]

Still, it's not the site's content that was adjudicated by the courts that granted *Rebel News*'s debate accreditation. It was the definition of journalism.

The debates in question were convened by a commission appointed by the government of Canada. For the 2019 federal election, the commission had asked the Parliamentary Press Gallery to review applications for accreditation; one day after receiving the formal request, the Gallery's secretariat responded with a note to *Rebel News* that read:

Hello,

Your request for media accreditation for the 2019 Federal Leaders' Debates has been denied. It is our view that your organization is actively involved in advocacy.

Regards, …[26]

The court found, among other things, that the decision process was "neither justified nor intelligible" and lacked "discernible rationality and logic." Particularly: "It is not apparent from the decisions or the mandate of the Commission why advocacy would disqualify one from accreditation."[27]

24 Galas, 'The Independence Party Hosts Leadership Debate'.
25 Saunders, 'Opinion'.
26 Lawton v. Canada (Leaders' Debates Commission), 2019 FC at 11.
27 Lawton v. Canada (Leaders' Debates Commission), 2019 FC at 32–33.

To the contrary, the judge noted that some of the accredited news organizations had editorially endorsed electoral candidates and parties, and that one, the *Toronto Star*, included the following within its published mandate (with emphasis as in the judgment):

> The Toronto Star is a multiplatform news organization that makes things happen. We inform, connect, investigate, report and *effect change.... We focus public attention on injustices of all kinds and on reforms designed to correct them.* We are the news organization people turn to when they need help; when they want to see the scales balanced, wrongs righted; when they want powerful people held to account.
>
> The Star has long been guided by the values of Joseph E. Atkinson, publisher from 1899 to 1948.... These values and beliefs now form what are called the Atkinson principles, the foundation of the Star's ongoing commitment to investigating and *advocating for social and economic justice.*[28]

For the next election, the debates commission adopted a more robust, two-stage procedure to avoid accusations of arbitrary discrimination. First, it granted automatic accreditation to members of the Parliamentary Press Gallery, to members of the country's two leading associations of journalists, and to the employees of publishers that belonged to Canada's two press councils. For other applicants, such as students and foreign correspondents, the commission would evaluate, case by case, whether the applying news organization produced work that measured up to the ethical guidelines of the Canadian Association of Journalists (CAJ).

The process was now clearly more fulsome and transparent, and when *Rebel* filed its new court action, the commission was ready with a comprehensible explanation: *Rebel*'s representatives would be in "conflict of interest" according to the CAJ guidelines because the website was engaged in advocacy on current political issues. The evidence: six petitions and funding appeals on the site opposing Covid-19 vaccine requirements, backing the return of a former prime minister, and other populist causes.

It was a nice try, but the new judge found the commission had unfairly created two classes of applicants and failed to "exercise

---

28 Lawton v. Canada (Leaders' Debates Commission), 2019 FC at 36–37.

its independence" over the process. More substantively, she found the advocacy of strong opinions to be consistent with journalistic functions:

> The Applicant cast this issue in terms of freedom of the press and the ability to put critical questions to the leaders of the vying political parties… There is room in the nation for the expression of opposing points of view. The Applicant did not ask to impose its views, but for the opportunity to participate in coverage of matters of importance during a federal election.[29]

If nothing else, the various cases of *Rebel News v. Canada* drew attention to the public-policy need for clear definitions of *journalism* and *journalist*. Nor does the need stop at accreditation questions. In Canada, as in a growing number of other democracies, the prize for recognition as a journalistic outlet can be cold, hard cash.

Because paying journalists to gather factual information of public interest is more expensive than making stuff up, many news brands have buckled to the disruptions of rerouted advertising dollars and free news sources. Cities that used to host multiple news outlets now have few; towns that had few now have one, or none. As a result the political and business leaders of towns, districts, and cities face less of the scrutiny that a free press is meant to guarantee. But even within the surviving "traditional" media, subject matter is skewed toward topics that attract the "clicks" which in turn produce the advertising revenues that can stave off an otherwise certain death. In such a situation, the argument for taxpayer-funded support is strong. As Stephen Gillers, a New York University law professor, argued with particular reference to investigative reporting:

> Press exposure of public and private conduct that is (or may be considered) wrong, hypocritical, abusive, harmful, or illegal (collectively, "wrongdoing") is necessary for democracy to work and is, therefore, a public good. The public should help pay for it.[30]

---

29 Rebel News Network Ltd. v. Canada (Leaders' Debates Commission), 2022 FC at 40–51.
30 Gillers, *Journalism under Fire*, 151–59.

The idea of government-funded news production is not novel. Many countries have operated public news services since soon after the invention of radio. Privately owned news organizations have long received financial relief of various kinds in various places, including postal discounts and various kinds of tax credits for journalists, publishers, advertisers, or subscribers. But disruption has dramatically broadened the case for aid.

At time of writing, Canada's Liberal Party government was routing about a quarter of a billion dollars a year to privately owned news media. The funds included various tax credits benefiting "qualified Canadian journalism organizations" and an industry-run grants and internship program that, in its first two years, hired 777 journalists to cover local communities and underreported issues.[31]

The advent of this suite of programs for saving news media sparked a paradoxical set of disputes amongst political parties, policy wonks and journalists themselves. The paradox: what divided the programs' supporters from their opponents was a principle on which they all seemed to agree: safeguarding the independence of the press!

The "pro" side had dire numbers on its side. In the ten years ending 2021, 423 local news outlets closed across Canada, and only 172 opened—a net loss of more than two news titles per month.[32] In the words of the most influential policy case for dramatically increasing government funding:

> [C]ivic engagement—local, provincial, regional and national—has so far shown itself to be most vulnerable to the disappearance of news outlets.... Anyone who views news as a public good will see that this decline damages civil discourse. Democracy relies on shared information—on all of us having access to news about what is going on in our communities.[33]

The opposing case was made by many journalists who have, against their own interest, firewalled themselves from government

---

31 Lindgren, Wechsler, and Wong, 'The COVID Years: Risk, Reward and Rethinking Priorities'.
32 Lindgren and Corbett, 'Local News Map Data - January 2022'.
33 Greenspon, 'The Shattered Mirror', 81.

funding. An editorial in a small but widely respected political newsletter, *The Line*, put it this way:

> ...There is no way to create such a system [of allocating financial support] without an inherently political process to answer philosophically fraught questions like "what is news?" and "what is a journalist?" And that takes us ever closer to the perilous path of state credentialization of a profession that only operates properly when it is free of both undue government interference and of government assistance. State meddling is bad for journalism whether the intent be good, bad or indifferent.[34]

Indeed, a form of "state credentialization" was created, in 2020, when the federal revenue agency appointed an advisory board of journalism experts to adjudicate organizations' eligibility for public support as news providers. The board reviewed more than two hundred applications for the status of a "qualified Canadian journalism organization" in its first two years of operation; both the applications and their outcomes were deemed confidential tax information, but it's clear most were successful.[35]

Perhaps inevitably, *Rebel News* applied to be "qualified" in this way, was denied, and launched a judicial appeal.[36] At time of writing, the matter has not yet reached a court.

Information Disorder and the New "News"

As a teenager and young adult, Malala Yousafzai was admired by practically everyone outside the Taliban as a fighter for Afghan girls' right to equality in education. A bullet in the head couldn't stop her, and she went on to win a Nobel Peace Prize. But she faced disapprobation soon after graduating from Oxford, when, in a Facebook post, she came out as a friend and admirer of a prospective leader of the university's Conservative students' association. Although she added that the endorsement was "not

---

34 'Dispatch from the Front Lines'.
35 'Independent Advisory Board on Eligibility for Journalism (2020–21)'; 'List of Qualifying Digital News Subscriptions'.
36 'Rebel News Is Suing Justin Trudeau'.

a reflection of [her] personal political views," retribution was swift: with OMGs and expletives aplenty, she was condemned as a "disingenuous careerist," an imperialist, and, indeed, a Conservative. Some professed shock; some said they'd known all along something was off; some demanded her deportation from the United Kingdom.[37]

An equivalently sharp repudiation of so seemingly mild an offence would be hard to imagine without social media's aptitude for forming "filter bubbles" or "echo chambers" in which users receive information that confirm and harden their own inclinations.[38] Eventually, this homogenization of perspectives punishes interest in alternative opinions while rewarding the humiliation of gotchas and ghosting in an often-terminal stasis that journalist Amanda Ripley terms "high conflict"—a spiralling, intractable polarization in which the value of mutual association dwarfs the originating issues of disagreement.[39]

We humans don't need technology to make us narrow-minded or to facilitate what has come to be called fake news: it's just natural to rely on those we already trust when it comes to determining what to believe. Especially in stressful times, we are apt to lose confidence in rational debate on things we feel deeply about; instead, we may find more comfort in connecting with people who are, or seem to be, congenial and who largely share our ideas.

Time spent with like-minded people is time *not* spent listening to those who seem different. This limits our ability to be surprised by facts, and social platforms make matters worse by luring us to spend even more time than in some previous eras with connections built on shared interests. The structures and cultures of these platforms actively discourage us from listening to nuance; rather, we are pulled to share and like what's familiar, and shush and cluck over what's alien.

And then, it gets worse: hate blooms. The difficulty of parsing correlation and cause—plus millennia of history replete with mob

---

37 Moore, 'On Social Media Everyone Is a Hero or Zero'; Wright, 'Nobel Peace Prize Winner Malala Yousafzai Is Trolled on Social Media'.
38 Cinelli et al., 'The Echo Chamber Effect on Social Media'; Flaxman, Goel, and Rao, 'Filter Bubbles, Echo Chambers, and Online News Consumption'.
39 Mounck, 'Https'; Haidt and Lukianoff, 'The Polarization Spiral'.

rule—should caution us against blaming all political polarization on social media, but evidence suggests that what begins as xenophobic discourse on the Internet can end in violence against people in blame-attracting groups—racialized people, immigrants, those of diverse genders, public health officials.[40] There has never been a global shortage of people to hate.

From Pluralism to Chaos

The end of the era of journalists' gatekeeping over news, and of the era of news publishing as a financial bonanza for corporations, could have been a net positive. Long before the word disruption came into use, Noam Chomsky recognized the problem for democracies posed by the control of public information by those he termed "elites."[41] UNESCO's first complete statement on freedom of the press, the Windhoek Declaration of 1991, declared that a free press must not only be independent of governmental, political or economic control, but also "pluralistic," defined as:

> ...the end of monopolies of any kind and the existence of the greatest possible number of newspapers, magazines and periodicals reflecting the widest possible range of opinion within the community.[42]

By this raw measure, digital disruption could have brought a golden age for the free press—a return to its Enlightenment roots, a time when millionaires and mavericks alike may reach mass audiences in a wild-west media market that shades both outlaws and cowboys and provides ample thorns to prick the corrupt sheriffs, the merciless bankers, and the respectable of all faiths. Not only commentators of all stripes but small-scale niche publishers and specialized reporters could use digital publishing's low-cost liberty to draw international, national, and local followings. Easier-to-use platforms offering the prospect of comfortable livings emerged with subscription newsletters giving freelancers

---

40 Müller and Schwarz, 'Fanning the Flames of Hate'; Williams et al., 'Hate in the Machine'.
41 Herman and Chomsky, *Manufacturing Consent*.
42 'Declaration of Windhoek', 2.

hopes for autonomy that would have been rare in the twentieth century.[43]

Unfortunately, these symptoms of apparently healthy pluralism hid the web-borne pathogens of what came to be dubbed information disorder. The name, coined in a 2017 report for the Council of Europe, aptly describes the pathological transmission of false or harmful messages originated by people and groups for purposes that aren't always consistent with truthfulness. The report's authors, Claire Wardle and Hossein Derakhshan, identified three types of problematic dissemination:

> Mis-information: the sharing of false information with no harmful intent.
> Dis-information: knowingly sharing false information to cause harm.
> Mal-information: sharing genuine information to cause harm, often by breaching privacy.[44]

The prevalence of all three types of disordered information challenges an assumption on which liberals have relied since the time of Mill: that truth evolves through people being presented with a free choice of what to believe or agree with. During the Covid-19 pandemic, widely circulated dubious theories challenged efforts to promote science-based defences of public health.[45] Given the problem's scale, some questioned the fitness for purpose of anti-censorship assumptions amidst ubiquitous verisimilitude.[46] As L.M. Sacasas, a technology analyst, put it:

> Whatever view you want to validate, you'll find facts to support it. ... [D]igital plenitude no longer sustains the hope that the truth will win out in the marketplace of ideas. Information super-abundance renders implausible the traditional ideal of

---

43 Oremus, 'What Substack Is Really Doing to the Media'; Smith, 'Why We're Freaking Out About Substack'; Smith, 'Heather Cox Richardson Offers a Break From the Media Maelstrom. It's Working.'
44 Wardle and Derakhshan, 'Information Disorder', 5.
45 See, for example: Chen et al., 'The Prevalence and Impact of Fake News on COVID-19 Vaccination in Taiwan'; Das and Ahmed, 'Rethinking Fake News'; Fleerackers et al., 'Communicating Scientific Uncertainty in an Age of COVID-19'.
46 Bechtold, 'Free Speech in America'.

the citizen as well-informed, critical thinker. Instead, it fosters the desire for tools that give users the ability to selectively censor their feeds, and the instinct to rely on moderators to restrict speech so as to conform with their values.[47]

Freedom Hurts

You and I may agree, and so might millions more, that life would get better if the Internet's doses of lies, threats, and hate were reduced. We might look expectantly to the "harm principle," which always lurks backstage when free expression gets out of hand, ready to spotlight a case for censorship. But that hope is misplaced. The likelihood of people getting hurt by what others say is not so much an avoidable risk as a cost that was, long before the birth of Facebook, baked into our way of life—and by "our," I mean "your," wherever you may be reading this. There is no "fix" for this except to replace democracy with tyranny.[48]

Nor is a scaled-down version of censorship viable. It's tempting to require platforms to follow common-sense moderation rules that filter the worst poisons—outright lies, egregious hate—but even if we assume a shift toward socially responsible business objectives, effective screening of content demands reliable distinctions on a mass scale between truth and falsehood. That's a step well beyond banning posts from selected authoritarian regimes, conspiracy movements like QAnon, or sites like 4chan, because it's not just those usual suspects who spread disinformation. Even democratic governments have been caught doing it.[49]

Could we, at least, oblige information platforms to tweak their feeds a tad, not to censor undesired material but to raise the profile of legitimate journalism in news feeds? Might we imagine a kind of algorithmic gene therapy that promotes news posts by authenticated journalists at the expense of more dubious content sources? Even were such a law technically and constitutionally viable, it would seem contrary to the letter and spirit of press

---

47 Sacasas, 'The Analog City and the Digital City'.
48 Gershberg and Illing, *The Paradox of Democracy*, 14, 280.
49 Bellingcat Investigation Team, 'The Making of QAnon'; Nix, 'Facebook, Twitter Dismantle a U.S. Influence Campaign about Ukraine'.

freedom. It's one thing to ease newsgatherers' access to facts but quite another to offer a leg-up in the competition for information channels—the rule of law requires clear and fair criteria for allocating resources. Just as a debates commission can't arbitrarily keep advocates out of a scrum, nor can a platform privilege a supposed news report just because a journalist created it. After all, ... — oh, come now, is that a groan I hear from you, the reader? Have you guessed what's coming? The show-stopping, imponderable, tiresome question that makes everyone want to push its asker into a river: *Who is a journalist?*

Yes, that.

The Necessity of Definition

Maybe there once were reasons to think that someone might have a better claim to public attention than someone else *just because they are a journalist*. But not in the age of digital access, as Silvio Waisbord argues:

> Multidimensional news gatekeeping has positive democratic consequences. It lets "a thousand voices bloom" as legacy journalism is thrown off its perch as the arbiter of news and truth. Lay expertise is no longer suffocated by the imperious power of elites and science. Journalism embedded in technocratic visions does not permeate every corner of the public sphere.[50]

This logic forces a new and more radical question: if people no longer look to journalists as society's designated arbiters of factuality, why should journalists be allotted any positive rights at all? The standard answer, as I've argued above, has less to do with publication than with newsgathering—the perceived necessity that some people should be charged with, and facilitated in, the discovery of factual information of public interest. This is not only the best reason for retaining the various positive rights, but the obligation on which those rights are contingent.[51]

For the purposes of allotting positive rights, then, a "journalist" is someone engaged in newsgathering. But no sooner is

---

50 Waisbord, 'Truth Is What Happens to News', 1872–73.
51 Lichtenberg, 'Foundations and Limits of Freedom of the Press', 332.

this sentence put on the page than its weaknesses cry to heaven. If anyone who goes looking for information of public interest must be allowed to appeal a search warrant, protect confidential sources, and so on, the intended exception must swiftly become the rule. If we start imposing a subjective limitation, such as that this journalist must adopt a neutral position, or anything along those lines, then we are right back against the wall with the Canadian officials' "unintelligible" attempts at parsing the boundaries of advocacy.

Chapter 4 will explore the "neutrality" question in greater depth, but let's merely note here that newspapers' advocacy for varying causes has long been pivotal to what Jürgen Habermas dubbed "the public sphere."[52] While various media institutions and systems have evolved since then with various levels of tolerance for pluralism in ideas, they have often done so in close connection to political transformations and conflicts.[53] "Mainstream" newspapers in many countries have historically been, or still are, connected to political parties, movements, or ideals, and whether or not outright expressions of opinion are labelled as editorial or "opinion," readers rarely have difficulty intuiting a paper's political orientation.

If, then, the definition of *journalist* does not include neutrality, what *does* it include? A few countries have resolved such questions with a statutory or regulatory determination of journalists' status. A 1946 Argentine law, for instance, described professional journalists as "people who regularly perform assignments in daily and periodical publications and news agencies and receive material compensation."[54] Most members of the Council of Europe adopted statutory definitions of *journalist* either before or after its Committee of Ministers recommended doing so (in order to cement the protection of confidential sources). The committee itself defined *journalist* as follows:

> Any natural or legal person who is regularly or professionally engaged in the collection and dissemination of information to the public via any means of mass communication.[55]

52 Copeland and Schorr, *The Idea of a Free Press*, 101.
53 Hallin and Mancini, *Comparing Media Systems*, 62.
54 Amado and Waisbord, 'Divided We Stand: Blurred Boundaries in Argentine Journalism', 56.
55 'The Status of Journalists in Europe: Resolution 2213 of the Parliamentary Assembly of the Council of Europe', 1405.

In the former British Empire, legal confusion prevails when it comes to defining journalists' status. Tortuous efforts were made by the British parliament to exempt "journalistic" and "democratically important" content from online-safety legislation,[56] while a judge rejected the British Union of Journalists' submission that Wikileaks founder Julian Assange's mass exposure of secret documents was equivalent to investigative journalism.[57] In the antipodes, official attempts to distinguish between real journalists and wannabes have created a soufflé of:

> ... jurisdictional clashes, challenges to legislative amendments, appeals to higher courts, and confusion for regulators and practitioners alike. In Australia, recently legislated shield laws have resulted in different definitions across the country's various jurisdictions. ... In New Zealand, a High Court judgement overturned a lower court decision, to find that a blogger could be viewed as a journalist.[58]

There is no intelligible *prima facie* reason *not* to view bloggers as journalists, as courts in the United States have found quite consistently as they navigate self-described journalists' appeals to protect confidential sources or to overturn denied access to press galleries. Judges in these matters are apt to rely on their own lists of sometimes conflicting criteria (without necessarily citing sources): Is the content edited by another person? Does the reporter work full-time? Is a message board equivalent to a news publication?[59] The vaunted First Amendment protects "the freedom of speech, or of the press" but the second half of that guarantee became known as an "empty clause"[60] in the late twentieth century when the U.S. Supreme Court persistently declined to offer guidelines for recognizing a journalist or news publication beyond the mere presence of a process ("the exercise of editorial control and judgment").[61]

56 Dickson, 'Britain Tries to Work out What a Journalist Is'.
57 Ponsford, 'Julian Assange Verdict'.
58 Johnston and Wallace, 'Who Is a Journalist? Changing Legal Definitions in a de-Territorialised Media Space'.
59 Schroeder, *The Press Clause and Digital Technology's Fourth Wave: Media Law and the Symbiotic Web*, 148–53.
60 Cowan and Westphal, 'Public Policy and Funding the News'.
61 Miami Herald Pub. Co. v. Tornillo, 418 U.S. 241 (1974) at 258.

Courts in Europe have taken a similar position, preferring to focus on the function of *journalism* as a process rather than on *journalists* as a "class."[62] This trend encouraged researchers on both sides of the Atlantic to describe a nascent consensus on what constitutes the journalistic "function" or core activity, whether it is conducted with or without involving established news organizations.[63] (My own contribution was to define journalism as "the activities involved in an independent pursuit of, or commentary upon, accurate information about current or recent events and its original presentation for public edification."[64]) These so-called functional definitions may or may not have contributed to theory, but have not significantly helped resolve practical problems such as accreditation or eligibility for state support.[65] Meanwhile, a new idea has emerged of distinguishing between "professional" and "peripheral" journalists, or, more subtly, examining characteristics of journalists' identities, practices, and organizational structures to describe their degree of distance from core professionalism.[66] (Chapter 5 will have more to say on what professionalism means for journalists.)

Back in Canada, my home and that of protester-journalists, rebel-advocates, and myriad others who claim unrebuttably to be journalists, courts have thus far managed to resist poking at the definitional soufflé. Animal rights activists launched a constitutional challenge to Ontario's aforementioned definition of journalists for the purpose of access to agricultural facilities.[67] The federal law shielding journalists' confidential sources remains unchallenged to date, but a leading Canadian human-rights scholar has warned that without "urgent attention" to definitional questions, protections of the press may be constitutionally unsustainable.[68]

---

62 Hovlid, 'Finding a Judicial Definition of Journalism: A Challenging Exercise in the Digital Age', 215–17.
63 Stearns, 'Acts of Journalism: Defining Press Freedom in the Digital Age'.
64 Malik and Shapiro, 'What's Digital? What's Journalism?'
65 Lamer, *Press Freedom as an International Human Right*, 37.
66 Hanusch and Löhmann, 'Dimensions of Peripherality in Journalism'; see also Oller Alonso et al., 'Defining the Worlds of Journalism Study Sample'; Bernier, 'Understanding Journalisms'.
67 General Regulation under the Security from Trespass and Protecting Food Security Act, S.O. 2020, c.9, sec. 11.
68 Cameron, 'Section 2(b)'s Other Fundamental Freedom', 21.

For now, the soulless information machine runs on, feeding both news and "news" to consumers with engagement opportunities that match reality to their expectations. The machine doesn't care what's accurate, false, or questionable, and doesn't expect humans to care, either. The result marks a transformative moment in the evolution of practical epistemology—a precipitous decline in the value of facts. As Chapter 4 will demonstrate, this shift leaves news workers questioning their goals, methods, and ethics, and asking a question that's as old as human thought: *What is truth?*

4 Shifting Truths, Altered Missions

Abstract

This chapter shows how diversification of news-media forms and skills, and a transnational reckoning with identity-based power, challenge the core journalistic obligation to pursue and disseminate factual information of public interest. Traditional appeals to detachment or to a "discipline of verification" understate the range of influences under which journalists work, including external expectations and limitations as well as journalists' own experientially formed interests, preferences and assumptions. However, the strict evidentiary disciplines of second-generation fact-checking outlets such as the Buenos Aires-based Chequeado embody an aggressive, post-disruption renovation of truth-seeking and truth-telling. This new approach adds an explicitly activist layer to journalism's alliance with factuality through interventionist countering of disordered information without other ideological preference. While various forms of advocacy remain part of the broader journalistic repertoire, "standpoint epistemology" is irreconcilable with the accuracy-based standards that underpin claims to news-media autonomy.

This, Too, Is News: Journalism's Evolving Shapes

A white van arrives in a city-centre park and its crew, dressed all in black, unload tightly packed cartons. With flamboyant haste, they position brightly coloured, metre-high icons on a stage-sized cloth gameboard they've unrolled on the grass. A signboard is

DOI: 10.4324/9781003223146-4

chalked: *HOY 1530-HS LOS JUEGOS DE CHEQUEADO*. A grey-bearded, ruffled-haired man starts bouncing a giant multicoloured ball. He's dressed in a khaki work coat that somehow announces the presence of a clown. The ball bounces higher, higher, higher than the trees; other performers wander the plaza announcing the imminent start of *La Oca* –the Game of the Goose. Children pull at parents' wrists, a crowd gathers, the coated clown leads a raucous chant of ¡*Una!* ¡*Dos!* ¡*Tres!* and a wide-eyed child, with parental helping hand, launches a huge spongey dice block onto the board.[1]

This is what the publication of a major investigative journalism project can look like in the post-disruption age. In the central plazas of five Argentine cities in 2017, *Chequeado*, one of the world's oldest and most innovative dedicated fact-checking organizations, presented findings from a collaborative probe into progress on key public works. (How far had repairs come in La Plata following massive flooding four years before? Were gas lines safer in Rosario after an explosion that left eighty dead?) Typically, in each city, computer-engineering students had programmed a city map to show damage, disrepair, and improvements according to official sources; neighbourhood groups helped cross-check and supplement the mapped locations; high school students captured images at the mapped sites; and a professional journalist interviewed technical and planning experts to gauge the challenge and assess progress. The idea was not only to scrutinize the fulfilment of official promises, but to provide a broader range of people with experience in monitoring government integrity. The findings were not just published on the social web but presented directly in the public-park "games."

The live-event experiment was consistent with engaging people who did not routinely follow political news, but only a few hundred people showed up to play or watch the plaza-games. "We met part of our goal with reaching out to people who would not know about this subject," Olivia Sohr, *Chequeado*'s research head, told me. "But if tomorrow we had to think about a way to share

---

1 Chequeado, 'Los Juegos de Chequeado [The Chequeado Games]'; Nafría, 'How Argentine Innovators Created Chequeado and Made It a Global Leader in Fact-Checking'.

the results of an investigation, I'm not sure one or two weekend public events is the [most cost-effective] way of reaching those people."[2]

Sohr's job title is Head of Impact and New Initiatives, reflecting the path-breaking culture of many countries' free-standing fact-checking operations that have disseminated their reports through customized multimedia content for Facebook, TikTok, WhatsApp, TV channels and more. Mainstream and peripheral news publishers alike have shown equivalent aggression in seeking new audiences with new formats including diverse suites of newsletters, live blogs with a range of curatorial voices, user-generated content, YouTube channels, edgy tiny-staff Substack brands, and subject-specialized subscription- or advertising-based outlets covering politics, business, sports, entertainment, fashion, wellness.[3]

This myriad of formats is what news looks like in the 2020s. If journalism's roots go back, long before Gutenberg, to wandering heralds announcing the news to all who would listen, then finding audiences in their virtual spaces is part of the essence of the disrupted press. "We want to reach people who don't follow the news," *Chequeado*'s general director, Laura Zommer, has said. "To increase the cost of lying, we need millions of people to worry about it, not just academics, journalists or politicians."[4]

To increase the cost of lying: at first glance, it strikes the ear less as a journalistic purpose than a partisan political shot. But if we listen a bit closer, this particular taking of sides is not like voters choosing a party or football fans cheering for their team. It's more like cheering for a referee whose hand hovers near their pocket— *YES, ref: yellow card!*—without caring which team will pay the price of sin.

But, no, that's not quite right, either. The idea of fact checking, when it's taken dead seriously (which isn't always the case), is to place journalists on the referee's team in the video replay booth, scrutinizing the evidence: was this statement a lie (red card!), a

---

2 Unless otherwise noted, information about Chequeado is drawn from interviews with Olivia Sohr (in person, May 6th, 2022) and Laura Zommer (by telephone, April 19th, 2022) and several subsequent email communications.
3 Newman, 'Journalism, Media, and Technology Trends and Predictions 2022'.
4 Oliver, 'The Fight for Facts in the Global South'.

half-truth (yellow!), or something only a little bit bad (warning? penalty? free kick?), or even (wow!) the actual truth?

"Report Things as They Are"

For journalists to play on the ref's team is consistent with this book's core argument so far: that, by protecting those who gather and disseminate factual information of public interest, freedom of the press asserts the public's right to know what's going on.

The centrality of fact-finding is not, of course, a new idea—it's a near-universal ethical expectation of journalists[5] and close to the heart of most journalists' own sense of purpose. When twenty-seven thousand journalists in sixty-seven countries were invited to choose amongst statements to represent the "most important thing in your work," the most popular—by far!—was: "Report things as they are." Their most important roles, they said, were to be informers, reporters, educators, and also watchdogs, which suggests a preference for facts that critique powerful parties. In many cases those same journalists added more interventionist self-expectations, such as fostering social change, justice, and development.[6]

This is, perhaps, an awkward combination of claimed roles that have sometimes been seen as residing within distinct media cultures. According to a recent version of an ever-evolving comparative model, *monitorial* news cultures expect journalists to maintain some distance from ideological loyalties, while journalists in *interventionist* and *developmental* cultures are involved with promoting values attached to a particular mission.[7] But as in many economic sectors, a globalizing shift is at work amongst news workers. According to Thomas Hanitzsch, Folker Hanusch, and Worlds of Journalism Study colleagues, the evident cohabitation of factuality with interventionism in journalists' role understanding pointed:

---

5 Mieth, 'The Basic Norm of Truthfulness: Its Ethical Justification and Universality'; Christians et al., 'Toward a Global Media Ethics', 138.
6 Hanitzsch et al., 'Journalists' Views on Their Place in Society', 163–74.
7 Hanusch and Hanitzsch, 'Comparing Journalistic Cultures Across Nations', 295–300.

...to a—sometimes latent, sometimes acute—conflict between a professional understanding journalists were trained into, on the one hand, and a reality of journalistic practice, on the other. The ideal of journalists acting as detached observers and objective bystanders has been developed in newsrooms in advanced industrialized societies and has subsequently been exported to large parts of the non-Western world through institutional transfer, training, and education, as well as the diffusion of occupational ideologies.... [T]hese values have become the global gold standard of news production.[8]

The values and norms that people expect of one another or to which they themselves aspire are not the whole story of the choices they make in practice. News workers, particularly, are subject to a range of influences that may include organizational routines, economic and ideological systems within which they operate, the availability of sources and assumptions about their credibility, the resource demands of original research, media owners' financial interests, legal limitations, and public expectations.[9]

It would be a mistake to conclude from this plethora of influences that journalists' beliefs about their roles are irrelevant to their practices, or vice versa. A sense of consistency between one's actions and values provides psychological rewards[10] that, according to social psychologists, support a robust connection between what people say they value and how they behave.[11] Role orientation and role performance evolve dynamically within the institutions in which they work. What journalists "ought to do, what they want to do, what journalists do in practice, and what they say they do" are dynamically related to one another, as Thomas Hanitzsch and Tim Vos suggest:

---

8 Hanitzsch et al., 'Journalists' Views on Their Place in Society', 174–75.
9 See, for example: Donsbach, 'Psychology of News Decisions'; Preston, *Making the News*; Schudson, *The Sociology of News*, 123–27; Shoemaker and Reese, *Mediating the Message in the 21st Century*, 64–202.
10 Rokeach, *The Nature of Human Values*; Feather, 'Values, Valences, and Choice'.
11 Feather, 'Values, Valences, and Course Enrollment: Testing the Role of Personal Values within an Expectancy-Valence Framework'; Bardi and Schwartz, 'Values and Behavior'.

These categories, and their empirical representations, are related in a nexus where normative roles shape cognitive roles, which drive journalists' actual practice that, in turn, is subject to observation, perception, and the construction of role images. These narratives finally feed back into normative and cognitive roles.[12]

Chilean journalism scholar Claudia Mellado and international colleagues, in turn, have used content analysis to show how journalists' role performance may either reflect or filter role orientations across various related media cultures. For instance, the practice of a monitorial or "watchdog" role orientation may exhibit varying degrees of two "sub-dimensions":

> ...a *detached watchdog*—closer to a more passive voice of the journalist when scrutinizing those in power "by reflecting reality"—and an *interventionist watchdog*, in which the journalist "shapes reality in the journalistic account" by openly questioning, criticizing, and making the allegations to scrutinize those in power....[13]

To whatever extent journalists' collective role performance may echo, filter, or veil their orienting sense of purpose, that purpose clearly depends on a key assumption—that such a thing exists as factual information or, to put it bluntly, truth. Only where truth exists can journalists realistically be expected to distinguish facts from errors, opinions, or lies. But the disruptions of this century's early decades have rattled the recognizability of truth, thus shaking the very foundations of an independent press.

Is That a Fact? Now, It All Depends

As mentioned toward the end of Chapter 3, the first newspapers were aligned with the advocacy of political parties and movements

---

12 Hanitzsch and Vos, 'Journalistic Roles and the Struggle Over Institutional Identity'.
13 Mellado et al., 'Investigating the Gap between Newspaper Journalists' Role Conceptions and Role Performance in Nine European, Asian, and Latin American Countries'; Márquez-Ramírez et al., 'Detached or Interventionist?'

(as many still are). Nevertheless, sometime before the First World War, a new idea emerged, especially in Anglo-American news cultures. There, journalists' collective sense of professional identity evolved toward an independent stance to political and economic interests and a defining concern with factuality. A landmark often noted in this respect was the founding of *The New York Times* in 1896, with its declared commitment to an "objective" report of the day's news.[14]

Such grand claims were easily exploded by scholars and other media critics as amounting, at most, to rhetorical tricks and rituals.[15] By the late twentieth century, scepticism of media owners' profit motives had led many to dismiss journalists' claims to impartiality as quixotic at best and disingenuous at worst. (A British critic, David Edwards, deemed the entire idea "psychopathic."[16]) Less ambitious were aspirational calls for news gatherers to privilege verifiable facts that could be attributed to reliable sources, and to correct inevitable errors forthrightly. Such things amounted, in the influential phrase popularized by Bill Kovach and Tom Rosenstiel, to a "discipline of verification."[17] Evidence suggests that journalists' adherence to this norm is less rigorous than meets the eye, but the name stuck.[18]

On the other hand, the new century saw a rising emphasis on transparency and responsiveness to audiences. These notions were more suited than factuality to the dynamics and culture of social media. Where journalists got stuff wrong, well, they could rely on swift correction by audience members.[19] The pursuit of factual information was now considered a collaborative enterprise in which the role of news workers rested not on their credentials but on practical assets like experience, networks, their organizational and editing assets, and the simple fact that providing information about current affairs was a full-time job.

---

14 Schudson, 'The Objectivity Norm in American Journalism'; Anderson, Downie, and Schudson, *The News Media*, 55–57.
15 Tuchman, 'Objectivity as Strategic Ritual'; Patterson and Donsbach, 'News Decisions'; Schultz, 'The Journalistic Gut Feeling'.
16 Edwards, *Guardians of Power: The Myth of the Liberal Media*.
17 Kovach and Rosenstiel, *The Elements of Journalism*.
18 Shapiro et al., 'Verification as a Strategic Ritual'.
19 Hermida, 'Tweets and Truth: Journalism as a Discipline of Collaborative Verification'.

This switch was supposed to enhance journalists' credibility, but public scepticism grew; reporters' mistakes circulated widely while scrupulously true news stories were shared in distorted form.[20] The wizard's curtain had been swept aside to reveal the frailty of those who suddenly faced competition for control over what constituted news.

Enter the Audience

Until the current century, it was editors—the ones whom scholars dubbed gatekeepers—who decided what the public needed to know. Their judgements bubbled out of a stew of personal instincts, handed-down criteria, competitive forces, and retrospective knowledge of what had, in the recent and not-so-recent past, tended to be popular with audiences (as measured by broadcast ratings and/or newspaper readership data).[21]

Social media changed all that by multiplying the way people could get their news; soon the most prominent feature of many newsrooms' architecture became the analytics screens that provided, moment-by-moment, increasingly detailed accounts of what pages were being viewed and for how long on which platforms by which slices of news consumers. As a 2017 report on newsroom design concluded: "By installing prominent screens in the newsroom, audience behaviour becomes part of the work environment.... These insights are key to understanding audience behaviour and monetizing digital content."[22]

Focusing news decisions on ordinary people's choices brought what Emily Bell termed "fundamental" changes to the process of making news.[23] Audiences now slid ever-closer to the driver's seat of evaluating newsworthiness in a symbiotic process that Nicole Blanchett has termed "participative gatekeeping." Through real-time observation of how journalists in three countries applied audience data to selecting, deselecting, and curating news on social platforms, Blanchett concluded:

20 Solomon, 'When Wire Services Make Mistakes, Misinformation Spreads Quickly'.
21 White, 'The Gatekeeper: A Case Study in the Selection of News'; Harcup and O'Neill, 'What Is News?'
22 Coester, 'A Matter of Space'.
23 Bell and Owen, 'The Platform Press', 25; See also Napoli, *Audience Evolution*.

Audience data are not simply numbers—they are participatory mechanisms that represent human behaviour and, through a variety of technologies, enable the participation of the audience in editorial decision-making pre- and post-publication.[24]

For news media to manage this transformed process has required new skills, new jobs, and new workers. A reporter or news editor might now sit across a desk from a media developer, a cross-platform producer, or an engagement editor, and virtually share that desk with an algorithm and a robotic news writer.[25] Meanwhile, newsrooms in many countries saw generational swings with attendant shifts in types of work. The Worlds of Journalism Study found that a focus on hard news was more evident in countries "where a young and fluid workforce is led by a small group of older and experienced journalists, whereas in wealthier countries with an early and well-established mass media, more journalists work in soft news."[26] When that study was fielded in the mid-2010s, younger people's consumption of news would have included more vigorous grazing on platforms that reward the expression of points of view more than uncoloured facts.[27]

This tension between factuality and point of view is only the latest version of the diversity of sectors, movements, and interests that news publications have openly promoted. These include partisan policies and ideals such as national development, democratic participation, solving problems, or peace, although a parallel liberal tradition has equated quality journalism with separating news from commentary—thus expecting news reporters to adopt impartial positions on social and political issues that they covered.[28]

Critiques of impartiality got a boost as another audience expectation made its mark. With the rise of anti-racist alertness in the late 2010s, more diverse reporters were needed to cover

---

24 Blanchett, 'Participative Gatekeeping'.
25 Cohen, 'At Work in the Digital Newsroom'; Anderson, *Rebuilding the News*.
26 Josephi et al., 'Profiles of Journalists', 101.
27 Galan et al., 'How Young People Consume News'.
28 Shapiro, 'Evaluating Journalism', 147–150,156–158; Bogart, 'Reflections on Content Quality in Newspapers', 40.

previously unexplored territories and provide communities with a broader sense of representation.[29] Marginalized journalists, especially, called out traditions of impartiality as excuses for defending status-quo interests and promoting the voices of racially and gender-privileged power-hoggers.[30] Editors and publishers began to relax some barriers; journalists were now urged to declare, rather than hide, their biases and affiliations.[31] Understated stylistic habits gave way to more forthright language: a politician's habitual deceptions might now be named "lies" rather than merely offset with rebuttals.[32] The norms of clarity and transparency seemed ready to eclipse what seemed stubbornly outdated orientations toward detachment and comprehensive coverage.

Most recently, the term, "movement journalism" has been coined to encapsulate what journalist and activist Anna Simonton described as journalism in service of "people coming together to build the power of all people to collectively control the conditions of our lives and our communities." (This characterization could, perhaps ironically, apply equally well to the much more establishmentarian civic journalism movement of the 1990s.) Amongst other decidedly partial (that is, anti-impartial) practices, movement journalism prides itself on straight-talking, such as "calling white supremacist violence out for what it is and in-depth reporting that illustrates community power in opposition to hostile policy."[33]

It was to be expected that greater diversity of journalists' experiences, perspectives, interests, and journalistic missions should also seed diversity in norms of practice. But the late 2010s also brought a deeper, more philosophical dispute to bear on what it means to seek, find, or tell the truth. Suddenly, the very existence of facts, previously questioned only in science fiction and epistemology tomes, became a matter of opinion.

---

29 See, for example: Callison and Young, 'Attending to The Reckoning and the Voiceless'; Gallagher, 'Gender Inequality, Media and Development'.
30 Mattar, 'Objectivity Is a Privilege Afforded to White Journalists'.
31 Jones, 'Should Journalists Be Allowed to Protest?'
32 Borchers, 'Media Standards on Lies and False Statements Are Changing Fast'.
33 Schneider, 'What Does Movement Journalism Mean for Journalism as a Whole?'; Simonton, 'Out of Struggle'.

"Whose Truth Is This?"

That life in society requires a shared "presumption of truth" seemed a global foundation of journalistic ethics as recently as 2008,[34] but it has not aged well. Post-disruption, the more popular presumption seems to be that facts are reliable to the extent that they align with the prevailing ideas within one's actual or virtual community. As I grow disposed to believe that X is true and Y false, I grow suspicious of evidence in support of Y, especially if it's rejected by my fellow X-people, who view Y-people as disagreeable/dangerous. By declining to pay attention to the arguments and evidence for Y, I deny its proponents a place in "my" reality. Once, *ad hominem* was a fallacy, but now it's an evidentiary method. Soon, the question, *Is this true?* seemed subsumed by the refrain, *Whose truth is this?*

This call to subjectivity can be understood in two different ways: as a benign appreciation of diverse perspectives on asserted facts, or as the more radical notion that truth exists *only* within people's subjective experiences.[35] The latter idea has become known as standpoint epistemology, which political scientist Yascha Mounck (who is, relevantly, a White man), has described as follows:

> There are some important pieces of knowledge about oppression and injustice that members of oppressed minority groups tend to have. And because they know something about the world that I don't, and because it is very hard—perhaps impossible—for them to communicate the nature of those experiences perfectly to somebody who hasn't experienced them, this means that they have a greater insight into what should be done. And if we aim to create a just society, we should, in certain contexts at least, defer ... to how they think about the world.[36]

It seems fair to expect journalists to temper their apprehension of reality when people's experiences are dramatically unequal. At

---

34 Christians et al., 'Toward a Global Media Ethics', 147.
35 Anderson, 'Feminist Epistemology and Philosophy of Science'; Mounk, 'You Just Won't Understand!'
36 Mounk, 'You Just Won't Understand!'

the very least, this involves listening to a diversity of expressed perspectives on ambiguous events and providing the kind of rich truth that resembles real life better than a who-what-when reduction of police-blotter "straight news."

But standpoint epistemology goes further. It takes the term "post-truth" to be a simple, literal, descriptor of our age. As Silvio Waisbord has noted:

> Misinformation and contested truths are constitutive of today's dynamic, multi-layered, chaotic public communication.... Without sharing a common epistemology—a way of producing and conversing about knowledge, facts, convictions, errors, there are competing forms of truth-telling anchored in different premises. Post-truth communication denotes the perennial absence of conditions for citizens to concur on objectives and processual norms. When expression blossoms, truth inevitably becomes contested.[37]

At its most uncompromising extreme, standpoint epistemology shrinks to potential nothingness the sphere in which any facts can be separated from subjective assertions—that is, the sphere of verification. Bolstered by the simultaneous proliferation of cynically created "fake news," the post-truth challenge attacks the core claim of hard news' symbolic rhetoric—that real events can, indeed, be described in the form of a set of facts.[38]

By 2022, the editor of *The New York Times*, once the home and hearth of "objectivity," was riffing on Woodward and Bernstein's homelier aspiration[39] in describing his paper's job: it was to "come out with the best version of the truth, with your own political opinion held in check by editors and editing."[40]

This idea—that journalists, despite recognizing many differences of history, culture, subject matter, or business model, see themselves as engaged in distinguishing facts from non-facts—remains

---

37 Waisbord, 'Truth Is What Happens to News', 1871.
38 Adam, 'Notes Towards a Definition of Journalism'; Shapiro, 'Evaluating Journalism'.
39 Mullin, 'Read Carl Bernstein and Bob Woodward's Remarks to the White House Correspondents' Association'.
40 Malone, 'Dean Baquet Never Wanted to Be an Editor'.

the most intuitive understanding of what the press offers. It's a pragmatic position somewhere far south of certainty but yet well north of nihilism, as Aviv Barnoy and Zvi Reich found:

> Obviously, journalists don't have time and resources for philosophical reflections. Yet, as far as their verification habits and the reasoning behind them reflect, news reporters tend to place the epistemic bar on a low point, adhering to what epistemologists term an "anti-reductionist" approach..., allowing themselves to rely on sources most of the time by default, without any verification whatsoever, as long as there are no defeaters—"counterbeliefs or counterevidence" (Lackey 2006, 166), that invite verification.
> ...In fact, news reporters develop some levels of knowledge most of the time. They even manage to develop autonomous knowledge in some cases... [by] relying on a mixture of testimonies and evidence.[41]

Doubts about factuality's achievement could have complex implications for press freedom, a liberty whose public value rests on providing both accurate information and a wide range of opinions. But the matter is simplified by recalling, once again, the difference between negative and positive rights. Pluralism of perspectives provides more-than-adequate support for negative rights—that is, for the absence of censorship and of other constraints on editorial autonomy. But the claim of positive rights (reserved privileges), which news media "hold in trust for the entire population,"[42] is tougher to justify without its attached obligation to provide—yes, again!—accurate information on current affairs.

Were journalism's newsgathering approaches to stray from this core responsibility, there's no persuasive basis left for the freedoms it has won. But, conversely, if a free press's pulse beats to the rhythm of hard facts, the vital signs may be strongest where the heart of journalism lies in separating truth from lies.

---

41 Barnoy and Reich, 'The When, Why, How and So-What of Verifications', 2327–28.
42 Siebert et al., *Four Theories of the Press*, 101.

Taking Sides with Truth (A View from Argentina)

As in many democracies, the president of Argentina addresses the national assembly annually in a televised address on the state of the nation. As in many democracies, journalists—prominently including *Chequeado*'s fact-checkers—cover those addresses on high alert to correct deceptive statements. Shortly before the 2018 address by then-president Mauricio Macri, his office sent *Chequeado* an advance copy annotated with its information sources. Macri's successor declined to follow suit, but either way, *Chequeado* checks every verifiable claim, director Zommer told me, "and they know we'll be doing it."

Fact checking has long been regarded as a pre-publication process within journalism as best practised, but the earliest years of this century saw the emergence of *post hoc* fact-checking teams, often operating outside established news brands, and often on a non-profit basis. In the 2010s, the number of these dedicated outlets grew from "a handful" in the United States to more than three hundred worldwide.[43] Of these, *Chequeado* (the name means "checked" in Spanish) is among the oldest. It was founded in 2009 by a physicist, an economist, and a chemist united by frustration at the evident contingency of information about public affairs.[44] Ten years later, its staff complement approached forty, not counting several volunteers and part-time consultants, with a budget equivalent to over one million euros largely provided by individual, corporate, and NGO donors.[45] About half of its hires have had prior news-media training or experience; Zommer herself is a lawyer and former information-access official who came to this job from a major daily newspaper, *La Nación*, where she covered human rights.

On the day I visited *Chequeado*'s office in May, 2022, the website had just published its latest fact-check report under the usual,

---

43 Graves, 'Boundaries Not Drawn'; Moreno-Gil, Ramon, and Rodríguez-Martínez, 'Fact-Checking Interventions as Counteroffensives'; 'Database of Global Fact Checking Sites'.
44 Nafría, 'How Argentine Innovators Created Chequeado and Made It a Global Leader in Fact-Checking'.
45 Riera and Zommer, 'Using Fact Checking to Improve Information Systems in Argentina'.

strictly formatted headline consisting of a statement in quotation marks and its source. In this case, the federal minister of economy had claimed that 94 percent of current export categories attracted lower tariffs than when the government had been elected.[46]

At my request, Olivia Sohr walked me through the process behind this report, loading up the research record as we hunched over her laptop screen.

The minister's statement had been caught, a few days earlier, by the site's always-updating, partially bot-fed, database of assertions of fact that were being widely shared on social media. An editorial team determined it to be relevant for checking according to posted criteria that included the degree of virality and the subject matter's public significance—an easy call, as Sohr explained, because Argentine farmers (who harvest almost half of the world's supply of soy products) were currently protesting against a proposed tariff hike.[47]

José Giménez, a staff business reporter, took on the investigation. He followed *Chequeado*'s standardized (and publicly posted) eight-step process, which required consulting both official and alternative sources including the statement's originator (the ministry, in this case). He then considered the information's context before proposing a conclusion on its veracity to newsroom leaders.[48]

A swift email exchange ensued to determine the item's colour-coded rating of true (green), false (red), or any of six more subtly shaded scores: unverifiable (that is, no evidence exists by which to confirm or deny the statement), "true but," premature (*apresurado*), exaggerated, misleading (*engañoso*), and unsustainable (defined as reliant on unconfirmed, unevaluated, or methodologically flawed research).[49]

The team's conclusion: a bright orange ENGAÑOSO stamp—not false, because the government had, indeed, reduced tariffs on

---

46 Giménez, 'Martín Guzmán: "El 94% de las posiciones [arancelarias] hoy tiene una alícuota menor que cuando empezamos el gobierno"'.
47 See Iorio and Raszewski, 'Argentina Halts Export Registration for Soy Oil, Meal'.
48 'Método de verificatión del debate público'.
49 Riera and Zommer, 'Using Fact Checking to Improve Information Systems in Argentina'.

94 percent of export *categories*—but not true either, because, as Gimeñez's story explained, those categories:

> ...together represented 39% of the total value of exports in 2020, while the remaining 5.7% accounted for 61% of the value. Within this [smaller] percentage are agricultural exports, whose rates have not gone down since 2019 and, in some cases, have increased.[50]

The final step—ongoing while Sohr and I spoke—was to promote the report on social platforms, but in a counterintuitively studied way that forms an integral part of the *Chequeado* method. When an alleged fact is selected for checking, the database notes the platforms on which the original statement was circulated most virally; if it's found to be false or misleading, the rebuttal is posted on those same platforms, and nowhere else. In fact, if the misinformation has gone cold by the time of publishing a rebuttal, it won't be promoted at all! As Sohr explained, this is to avoid accidentally spreading the original misinformation:

> If we maybe do a debunk of something that's already kind of gone down in virality, we will not share it [widely] ... unless it's something incredibly serious that could harm people's health or something. We'll just leave it there [on the website] so that people can reach it when they Google it.

Actively *discouraging* readership is a unique approach to news publishing—as in, the polar opposite of clickbait! But it shouldn't be mistaken for apathy about audience size. *Chequeado* has made a point of enhancing discoverability with new formats, such as short audio clips for WhatsApp and for community radio stations, including some in Indigenous languages as part of a collaboration with other Latin American agencies. As Zommer told me:

---

50 Translated from: Giménez, 'Martín Guzmán: "El 94% de las posiciones [arancelarias] hoy tiene una alícuota menor que cuando empezamos el gobierno"'.

> We're not waiting for people to come to us.... We are looking all the time for ways to reach the attention of people who, in some cases, work twenty hours a day. They are exhausted. They don't want to receive bad news when they are traveling back home. We value their time and attention, so we use short formats; in some cases, we use humour, memes.

Studies of fact checking's impact on people's beliefs have shown mixed results, but there's some reason to think it changes their social-media behaviour by diminishing shares of false information.[51] This seems true for people with a variety of political beliefs, although actually sharing a fact-check report is more likely if it tends to confirm one's own attitudes.[52] A study commissioned by *Chequeado* suggested that rebuttals are less likely to be spread than validations, both "in the community aligned with such a story, as well as the disagreeing community."[53]

But in Argentina, at least, there's a suggestion that the polarization knot can be cut by securing a nonpartisan reputation for reliability. Both supporters and opponents of the government seem equally likely to receive and share *Chequeado*'s reports[54] and politicians themselves use its confirmations and rebuttals as campaign material.[55] Does this mean the job's done—that political deception has met its match? I asked Zommer whether she thinks Argentine leaders, of any political stripe, are less inclined to deceive people today than before *Chequeado* came along. She paused just a second or two, then said:

> I'm not sure they lie less, but they lie with less impunity. They know they can be caught. They know that someone can come tell them, "You're lying." The big lies that just passed unnoticed perhaps 15 years ago are today not passing in that simple way.

---

51 Aird et al., 'Does Truth Matter to Voters?'; Porter and Wood, 'The Global Effectiveness of Fact-Checking'; Ma et al., 'Fact-Checking as a Deterrent?'
52 Shin and Thorson, 'Partisan Selective Sharing'; Amazeen, Vargo, and Hopp, 'Reinforcing Attitudes in a Gatewatching News Era'.
53 Calvo et al., 'Chequeado in Argentina', 17–20.
54 Calvo et al., 27.
55 Riera and Zommer, 'Using Fact Checking to Improve Information Systems in Argentina', 602.

The Duties That Freedom Demands

Almost by definition, professional fact checking stands as an antagonist to standpoint epistemology. As *Chequeado*'s Laura Zommer made clear:

> In our country, we have something called *periodisme militante* [militant journalism], and for me, that is impossible. Sorry for that. Perhaps this is old-fashioned.... I think you should be transparent about your own personal beliefs, and put your audience in a better position to know your possible conflict of interest, but when you are reporting, you should be accurate and honest. And if not, you are doing PR, not journalism.

Perhaps "accurate and honest" resonates as (yes) "old-fashioned" impartiality or detachment, but not on closer examination. *Chequeado* is part of a growing movement of "second generation fact checkers," for whom checking the accuracy of individual claims is only a starting point for a larger, more ambitious mission, which is "to redress the impact of misleading and inaccurate information and to tackle the underlying problems of misinformation."[56]

With truth-promotion as a guiding principle, rather than mere truth-telling, these organizations campaign assertively for open access to official documents, demand corrections to public records, and mount educational events on media literacy.[57] It's simple good sense to create TikTok reels and data maps, to mount public events that spark awareness of political lies, and, yes, to sacrifice potential audience rather than oxygenate misinformation. At the time of this writing, the most prominent content on *Chequeado*'s home page was not the latest fact-checking report but the launch of a series explaining electoral systems, with an accompanying guide for electoral officers.

Similarly, in neighbouring Brazil, the fact-checking agency *Lupa* (Portuguese for "magnifying glass") rebranded itself in 2021 as a "hub to fight misinformation and disinformation." While it continues to produce text and videos that verify or rebut widely

---

56 Riera and Zommer, 600.
57 Africa Check, Chequeado, and Full Fact, 'Fact Checking Doesn't Work (the Way You Think It Does)'.

circulated statements, that's just one step in a mission "to educate people so they can recognise correct information when they see it."[58]

Seen in this expanded way, second-generation fact checkers arguably fit more easily under the heading of interventionists than of detached monitors. They are advocates—biased as all get-out!—but for a cause that's integral to journalism's core mission.

A "role obligation" is the name ethicists give to normative demands that apply to some people, but not others, based on the part they play in a community. You and I may agree that everyone should try to be kind to children, but also that parents owe additional duties of care toward *their* children. We don't get to pick and choose amongst those expectations; they come bundled with the newborn and bind us for life. The same, more or less, applies to health-care professionals' obligations toward their patients, or engineers' to public safety. The obligation doesn't arise from the taking of a vow or signing a contract, as Michael O. Hardimon argued:

> It arises simply because one occupies a particular role given that certain moral background conditions are in place (for example, that the institution is just and that the role is reflectively acceptable). Superstar lawyers may be able to name their own price, but what it is to be a lawyer is something no lawyer can settle. Social roles are not things that we, as individuals, make up…. We, as a society, have defined and continue to define them in a particular way.[59]

Let me assume, as the rules of rhetoric demand, that by now I have persuaded you that journalists, by reason of their career choice, have taken on a core obligation to serve the cause of truthfulness. Your next question may be: So, what? What difference should this make to news work?

Day to day, perhaps, not much. The core obligation by no means rules out journalists' applying other, complementary, motivating values in their work. They draw on their perspectives, experiences, and beliefs every time they propose, select, report, produce, or

---

58 Zaffarano, '[Interview] Marcela Duarte: Head of Product - Agência Lupa'.
59 Hardimon, 'Role Obligations', 350–55.

present the news. Acknowledging a *primary* social role of fact-seeker and truth-teller doesn't especially narrow or broaden the range of available news choices, just so long as none involves messing with facts. As Hardimon pointed out, it is:

> ...possible for reasonable individuals to interpret their social roles in unconventional ways... There are different ways of being a flight attendant, oncologist, and police officer. Part of what it is to become a good flight attendant, oncologist, or police officer is to find a way of carrying out the responsibilities of these roles which suits one's particularities. All this being said, it remains true that individuals cannot custom tailor the obligations they undertake in entering contractual social roles. To the extent that a role contains options, those options are fixed by the role. To sign on for a role is to sign on for the whole package, properly understood.[60]

Part of that package for journalists is, I suggest, a bunch of barbed question marks directed at ritualistic half-measures that have often passed for verification in practice. A corroborating source (or ten of them) doesn't make a false assertion true and, conversely, failing to find supporting evidence doesn't make the assertion false. Sources become available mostly if they have an interest in being available—which isn't the same as their having an interest in accuracy. Some truths have never been documented; some documents will never be found. A habit of relying on knowledge that's at hand, rather than seeking differing perspectives and tackling complexity, amounts to a bias towards what's familiar and against what's foreign.[61] By contrast, it is journalists' collective job to be critical of inherited assumptions, protocols, and short cuts, subjecting all assertions to tests of credibility that are, if not perfect, at least better than, "This is the way we do it here."

Viviane Fairbank, a graduate student of philosophy who used to be a fact checker for leading magazines, puts it this way:

> Journalism is not only about getting facts right—it's also about deciding which facts can be confirmed in the first place, which

---

60 Hardimon, 355.
61 Benton, 'This Report Sees Journalistic "Bias" Less as Partisanship and More as Relying on Too-Comfortable Habits'.

ones we choose to include in our reporting, and whom we consider fit to assess them.... We need some way of insisting on the existence of truth while acknowledging that its boundaries are blurry—that it is reasonable, even necessary, to push against them sometimes. One of the greatest hurdles to this realization is our stubborn separation of rationality from emotion, a distinction that both sides of the political spectrum rely on. People on the left will often say it is the right's stubborn belief in a preferred alternative reality and its surrender to emotions of fear that lead it to problematic views and conspiracy theories. But people on the right use the exact same rhetoric as those on the left.... Both sides believe they are the ones best suited to make informed decisions based on available facts, and each judges the other for being incapable of doing the same.[62]

Acknowledging their core obligation should also help journalists, somewhat, in questions of ethics. Role obligations don't turn ethical dilemmas into absolutes (partly because human beings don't shuck off their ties to humanity when they accept a job) but where those dilemmas involve a choice between truths and lies, a journalist's bias should be clear. *Chequeado*'s policy against expanding the audience of false information carries implications for journalists' news choices universally—no matter who told the lie first. If this seems obvious to you, you may not have been paying attention to political news for the past decade or so. (Lucky you.)

A further, perhaps also-obvious implication: there is no persuasive way to reconcile a bias toward factuality with standpoint epistemology. *Whose truth is this?* may be a fine trope for activists and advertising agents, but she-said-they-said won't help a journalist defend a lawsuit for libel, and it's no way to make a case for press freedom. As investigative journalist Heather Brooke put it:

> Professional journalism has one real Unique Selling Point in the digital age, one reason why anyone would want to get their news from a professional journalist rather than anywhere else: the ability, gained through training and experience, of sifting

62 Fairbank, 'How Do We Exit the Post-Truth Era?'

through mounds of information for what is a) important and b) verifiable or as true or as close to the truth as possible.[63]

A Case For Autonomy With Standards

In a 2020 UNESCO report, Marius Dragomir suggested that an independent press requires guarantees for editorial autonomy combined with meaningfully monitored professional standards. He explained:

> [J]ournalism needs to be autonomous of external influences that violate its precepts and protocols. At the same time, it needs institutional guardrails in order to ensure that it lives up to its professional standards and is protected from internal threats.
>
> There are risks that an emphasis on autonomy alone can lead to a situation in which individuals who claim to be doing journalism decide for themselves what journalism is, in ways that do not adhere to professional and ethical standards. At the same time, without autonomy, there is the risk of the instrumentalization of media, where journalists end up transgressing professional standards due to serving certain vested interests rather than the public interest. What mediates these tensions is the recognition that editorial independence is not an end in itself, but rather it goes hand-in-hand with the boundaries established by professional standards. Journalism produced by news institutions depends on both of these elements.[64]

If this argument seems hard to grasp, it may help to recall the unprecedented range of threats that disruption brings to bear on an independent press—threats that may come from surprising people. A media owner may have bought in to seed quality journalism but now needs to recoup losses. State grants may look like rescue craft until their empowering regulations become gunboats. Philanthropists may harbour hidden expectations; social platforms' pay-outs may leave niche news outlets high and dry; journalists'

---

63 Brooke, *The Revolution Will Be Digitised*, 70.
64 Dragomir, *Reporting Facts*, 8.

own failures may sink local audiences' trust to the point of collapse. These threats wax or wane in various rhythms in different countries, especially as power shifts amongst the institutions and dynamics that foster or endanger autonomous journalism. In places where publishers have worried most about censorship, the imminent nightmare may become financial collapse. Elsewhere, the threats that preoccupy journalists relate to psychological and physical safety.

As Dragomir argues, some of these threats to autonomy could well be mitigated by grounding the rights of news workers on robust self-regulation according to professional norms. But many journalists, jealous of their *individual* autonomy, will see a paradox in reliance on "institutional guardrails" to foster *professional* independence. If a sword exists to cut this knot, it might be found in a country that has nearly a century of experience with self-regulated news media. On to Chapter 5; destination: Norway.

5 A Profession Whose Time Has Come

Abstract

This chapter discusses the correlations of press freedom with editorial autonomy and professional accountability. Where editorial autonomy exists in the richest sense, two conditions are met: governments, businesses, and other powerful interests are impeded from interfering with news content and processes; and journalists' choices are subject to peer-approved professional standards of public service. In Norway, where both these conditions are especially evident, the general public has historically demonstrated strong trust in journalists' autonomy and maintain high levels of commitment to paying for news. Recent years have seen journalists and stakeholders in diverse democratic systems and cultures move closer toward a nascent global consensus on the profession's foundational goals and values, but performative half-measures are easier than building muscular provisions for professional autonomy and accountability. Such accountability need not compromise pluralism across cultures, sectors, and viewpoints. Some elements contained in legal defences for defamation suggest a nascent global consensus on standards of "responsible journalism."

Where Local News Blooms

"Have you ever heard of news deserts?"

As the question escaped my lips, it sounded almost offensive. But Sigurd Haugsgjerd had been unflappably polite since I arrived (late, flustered, sleep-deprived by the persistent Nordic June sun) for morning coffee, and his bright blue eyes did not blink now.

DOI: 10.4324/9781003223146-5

78 *A Profession Whose Time Has Come*

"*Nei*," he said. "What's that?"

Nothing, for sure, like this. Nothing like the village of Bygland or the other rural communities squeezed between blue-white water and steep granite cliffs in the southern Norwegian valley of Setesdal. The valley gets local news from *Setesdølen*, the community newspaper that Haugsgjerd owns and edits, and regional news out of the south coastal city of Kristiansand, home to public and private TV and radio stations plus a fist-thick daily paper, *Fædrelandsvennen* that employed (in November, 2022) fifty-five unionized journalists and a total staff around one hundred and boasted thirty-five thousand subscribers (digital and print combined).[1] The entire county's population is around three hundred thousand.

In my part of the world, North America, a paper with equivalent-sized target audience would be lucky to employ half as many journalists as *Fædrelandsvennen*.[2] Somewhere in the United States, a community newspaper editor is likely drafting a farewell to readers as I sit writing this sentence; the million-plus residents of suburban Montgomery County, just north of Washington, DC, saw their last newspaper, a weekly, shut up shop in 2020.[3]

But this is Norway.

Ninety minutes' drive north of Kristiansand, up along the Otra river through spiny forests and gorge tunnels, stands the ranch-house style office of *Setesdølen*. Its two weekly editions (Tuesdays and Fridays) include about twenty-four news pages, mostly dominated by photos of community members over a steady news diet of family and school reunions along with community, sports, and church events; every confirmation service in every parish is marked by a photo as a matter of editorial policy. And then there's local politics, local business, the occasional fire or crime, or the opening of a new facility. The editor himself writes a short, acerbic column on Page 2 that betrays no hesitance about calling out business, political, and religious leaders for what he considers

---

1 Data provided by Janne B. Prestvold, who leads the *Fædrelandsvennen* unit of the National Union of Norwegian Journalists and is a member of the union's national board. Except where otherwise cited, information in this chapter relies on interviews I conducted in Bygland, Kristiansand, and Oslo, June 1–3, 2022.
2 Estimate by this author based on sampling research conducted by the Canadian Worlds of Journalism Study.
3 Abernathy, 'News Deserts and Ghost Newspapers', 16–17.

unfair decisions, intolerant positions, or insufficient attention to the valley's best interests.

Apart from Sigurd Haugsgjerd, the rest of the editorial staff at the time of my visit consisted of his son, Olav (a journalism graduate who has worked for the national public broadcaster, NRK) and daughter, Sigrid (a New York-trained photographer who works here as part-journalist, part-general manager). The all-in-family approach is recent, but the newsroom complement has been constant at two to three for decades. Readership has stayed steady as well. When I asked for an update, Olav pulled the current numbers off his phone: the newspaper reaches 3,411 subscribers, and 486 more pay for digital access only.

About four thousand paying subscribers isn't much, but that's local journalism for you. And the valley's population? Roughly six thousand, Olav said, from memory, "including everyone from retirement home to kindergarten, so probably about two thousand households."

"I'm sorry," I said, frowning up from my notes. "That's—?"

Olav nodded, yes: that's twice as many subscriptions as households. His father explained, speaking for about two minutes in Nynorsk (the country's second official language, but the valley's first). Olav translated this much: "Many people move away and want to stay in touch with their home. And the tourists [city-living weekenders] subscribe as well." The paper is printed on the coast and delivered next day not only in the valley but as far away as Oslo. "And then, a lady from the retirement home comes to pick up a copy and reads it aloud for the people that have bad eyesight."

Not a news desert, then.

Here, you might (unless your own origins lie in Europe's polar lands) sigh: *Ah, but that's Norway*. And it's true that Nordic countries sit routinely, predictably, and (to the rest of us, if we're honest) annoyingly atop almost every international index of health and happiness.[4]

And wealth-wise, yes, Norway's oil provides top-ten prosperity,[5] which helps pay for expensive goods, such as journalism.

---

4 Pinsker, 'We're Learning the Wrong Lessons From the World's Happiest Countries'; 'Happiness, Benevolence, and Trust During COVID-19 and Beyond'.
5 'GDP per Capita (Current US$) | Data'; Rauhala, 'Norway Is Portrayed as Both Hero and Villain in Europe's Energy Crisis'.

But neither wealth nor happiness seems adequate to explain the trend-defying high news readership in every Norwegian age group or the extraordinary proportion of 41 percent of Norwegian online news consumers who said, when surveyed for the Reuters Institute, that they paid for online news content. (Swedes were second at 33 percent, with all other surveyed countries well below 20 percent.)[6]

Since advertising follows eyeballs, the continuing commercial success of Norwegian news products[7] begins to seem less surprising. *Setesdølen*'s back issues show little change over the decades in advertising content over the past few decades: full pages offer cars and farm equipment, announcements from banks and real estate agents, and stacked display ads such as have all but disappeared from print elsewhere. The ads come steadily, it seems, despite the paper's history of exposing business influence on local politics, sometimes illustrated by cartoons showing variations on a theme of overweight money-bag holders kicking mayors' hindquarters.

I asked Sigurd Haugsgjerd if businesses sometimes withdraw advertising to protest against his paper's reporting.

"*Nei*," he said, smiling.

I pressed. Truly? Not once, in nearly five decades?

"*Nei.*"

But sometimes such a thing is threatened?

"*Nei, nei.*"

"What do you make of that?" I asked finally.

The editor gazed down, for a moment or two, at the desk between us, and then he almost winked as he said, surprisingly in English: "Maybe we haven't been tough enough." And chuckled.

"Do you actually think that?"

He cleared his throat, dropped the smile, and switched to Nynorsk, which translated thus: "I don't remember any situations where my integrity has been compromised. Maybe I could have been sharper to the big business owners, but, on the other hand, there are not many big businesses around here."

---

6 Newman et al., 'Digital News Report 2022'.
7 Puijk et al., 'Local Newspapers' Transition to Online Publishing and Video Use'; Slaatta, 'Print versus Digital in Norwegian Newspapers'; Hatcher and Haavik, '"We Write with Our Hearts"'.

Ingredients of Autonomy

Integrity is a word that Sigurd Haugsgjerd uses quite a lot, not just in our conversation but also in occasional interviews published in other centres. The word seems to mean to him what others sometimes call journalistic autonomy. According to UNESCO, it's an essential element of the freedom of the press and connotes:

> ...the extent to which media outlets and journalists are able to function separately from the government and other external interests, and where professional ethics enable them to perform their public service role, including that of being a watchdog.[8]

This description may be simplified as follows:

> *Journalists enjoy autonomy where their practice is directed by their own professional standards of public service rather than by the interests of other stakeholders.*

It follows that, as foreseen in the conclusion of Chapter 4, press freedom will thrive where *both* of two separate and interrelated conditions are satisfied. The first is the avoidance of external restraints: governments, businesses, and other powerful interests should be impeded from interfering with news content and processes. The second is the presence of internalized checks: journalists themselves should be constrained by peer-approved professional standards of public service in their processes for creating and providing news content.

Neither of these conditions is easily fulfilled, but deterring governments from interfering with journalists' autonomy is (as noted in Chapters 1 and 2) the chief reason for the inclusion of press freedom in constitutional charters. As for business interests, it's far from uncommon, in most countries, for owners of for-profit news businesses to retain influence over editorial direction, however discreetly this may be exercised. Tension between publishers and editors is unavoidable, even in non-profit and public-service organizations, and doesn't need to be unhealthy, but the scale's calibration will reflect, to some degree, journalists' sense of job

---

8 Ichou, *World Trends in Freedom of Expression and Media Development*, 66.

security and the extent to which union contracts cement adherence to journalistic norms.[9]

Digital disruption has increased the pace, stress, and commercial expectations imposed on journalists' work[10] and made their jobs more precarious, exposing them to what Greg de Peuter describes as an "existential, financial and social insecurity exacerbated by the flexibilization of labour markets."[11] Insecurity of this kind has cognitive and emotional consequences[12] to which journalists cannot be immune, especially in the absence of secure contracts and salaried positions.[13]

This brings us to the second condition for journalistic autonomy: the grounding of editorial integrity on professional standards of public service. To make this realistically achievable requires more than individual confidence *vis-à-vis* commercial pressures; it requires a set of collective standards that are actively pressed by peers in a stable, united professional association or union. In many settings, this notion presents a can of worms that must now be opened.

From Boundary Work to Professional Standards

The word *professional* has broad connotations, from a nod to workplace propriety in everyday parlance to the presence of the "occupational ideology" that Mark Deuze called "ideal-typical values."[14] In some journalistic milieux, varieties of the "p"-word have often elicited suspicion, or at least ambiguity. I've met several respected journalists who prefer to speak of their work as a "craft," not a profession, because of a wide resistance in many news cultures to any hint of self-regulation. Many journalists are, by nature, "non-belongers," a lifetime union leader once told me, and they especially resist conformity with what they see as rigid expectations. A newsroom steward might ignore the collective agreement's clause controlling job promotions because, as a

---

9 See Cohen and de Peuter, *New Media Unions*.
10 Cohen, 'At Work in the Digital Newsroom'.
11 de Peuter, 'Creative Economy and Labor Precarity: A Contested Convergence', 419.
12 Hardt and Negri, *Commonwealth*, 147.
13 Cohen, 'Cultural Work as a Site of Struggle'.
14 Deuze, 'What Is Journalism?'

journalist, they don't think the assessment of journalistic performance can be encoded. The union leader said he saw this as a kind of phenomenology: it was as if "merit was a revealed truth that was verified by peer reputation."

Columbia University's Michael Schudson was not just describing the journalists of his own country when he suggested their best work is done by following their most "unlovable" collective instincts:

> The focus of the news media on events, rather than trends and structures; the fixation of the press on conflict whenever and wherever it erupts; the cynicism of journalists about politics and politicians; and the alienation of journalists from the communities they cover make the media hard for people to love. But these are just the features that make journalism indispensable. These are the features that most regularly enable the press to exercise a capacity for subverting established power.[15]

"Unlovable" journalists of this kind are too self-consciously individualistic to accept being bossed around—even by peers, in the name of common ideals. On the other hand, journalists who do claim to be bound by professional norms have often been cast as engaging in self-aggrandizing rhetoric[16] or defensive discourse[17] that amounts to reputation-building "boundary work"[18]—that is, erecting fortress walls to exclude other information providers[19] including so-called interloper media.[20] Cogent arguments have been made that for journalists, professionalism endangers democracy[21] *and* that it fosters freedom;[22] that it promotes autonomy[23] *and* that it retards ethical conduct.[24]

---

15 Schudson, *Why Democracies Need an Unlovable Press*, 50.
16 Winston and Winston, *The Roots of Fake News*, 100–102.
17 Shapiro et al., 'Images of Essence', 42–43.
18 Carlson, 'Boundary Work'.
19 Lewis, 'The Tension Between Professional Control and Open Participation'.
20 Eldridge, 'Boundary Maintenance and Interloper Media Reaction'; Hujanen et al., 'Performing Journalism'.
21 Merrill, 'Professionalization'.
22 Hamada et al., 'Editorial Autonomy', 134–35.
23 Coddington, '"Glory and Honor"'.
24 Craft, 'Distinguishing Features'.

Can of worms, did I say? Make it a barrel. Journalists in liberal regimes may consider *professionalization* a slippery slope to state certification, which they assume would abrogate journalists' autonomy. But in authoritarian countries, *professionalism* implies almost the opposite: successfully maintaining standards despite state interference.[25] For survey sampling purposes, some researchers have identified *professional* journalists by weighing income sources, use of work time, or self-identification; others have seen this tactic as biased toward prosperity.[26]

Sociological theory offers more complex markers, preeminently including (in recent years) the *habitus* (loosely, practices) and *doxa* (norms) associated with Pierre Bourdieu's field theory.[27] But most broadly, professionalism suggests the presence of a collective orientation amongst people doing comparable work (in this case, news work) to largely shared ideas about role identity, occupational purpose, and values of public service rather than to the demands of external forces (such as audience preferences, political institutions, and business concerns).[28]

In a word: standards. But now a more specific question arises: how realistic is it to imagine large communities of journalists agreeing on robust rules to which they are ready to bind themselves?

Diverse Practices, Common Principles

Many journalists claim high awareness of social responsibility, of the effects of their work on individuals (such as sources), and of codes of ethics.[29] The details of such alignments can be highly diverse, both amongst national news systems and within them. A small community, for instance, may justly expect local news media to display local loyalties, though not extending to the point

---

25 Meng and Zhang, 'Contested Journalistic Professionalism in China'.
26 Oller Alonso et al., 'Defining the Worlds of Journalism Study Sample', 3,4,16.
27 Bourdieu, 'The Political Field, the Social Science Field, and the Journalistic Field'.
28 Hallin and Mancini, *Comparing Media Systems*, 33–41; Deuze, 'What Is Journalism?', 444–46.
29 Harro-Loit, 'Journalists' Views about Accountability to Different Social Groups'; Ramaprasad et al., 'Ethical Considerations: Journalists' Perceptions of Professional Practice'.

of xenophobia. Specific demands are likewise made of reporters, editors, commentators, audience-participation specialists, photojournalists, and those expected to energize followers by enlarging their online personalities.[30]

Other expectations are specific to subject matter: a business reporter is obliged to take precautions around influencing markets, and a cartoonist to avoid stereotypes, with a myriad of other norms applying to politics, business, sport, lifestyle, and so on.[31] Freelancers may operate under different rules from those bound by employment contracts.[32] Moment-by-moment online journalism typically operates to different expectations of, for example, comprehensiveness and correctability.[33]

Some differences flow from individual organizations' cultures. The publicly funded BBC has historically required its vast news staff to exhibit a degree of evident impartiality that would look just silly on a private channel's celebrity show or in a sports magazine.[34]

And yet, journalists often switch jobs with marginal dissonance—from a business-aligned news brand or public-service broadcaster, say, to a populist-inclined tabloid or a magazine that exhibits broad curiosity about life. Others, when migrating to a new country or continent, or between media platforms or organizations, will encounter significantly different role expectations.[35] Of the several journalists I have known who did exactly this, none has mentioned feeling as if they had changed careers, or sought retraining, or felt morally lost. If some didn't like their new environment, they moved back or moved on.

Around the globe, journalists are highly likely to claim awareness of social responsibility, of the effects of their work on individuals

---

30 Mellado and Hermida, 'The Promoter, Celebrity, and Joker Roles in Journalists' Social Media Performance'.
31 See, for example, Perreault and Miller, 'When Journalists Are Voiceless'; Hardin and Billings, 'A Fracturing Profession on Shifting Terrain'.
32 Josephi and O'Donnell, 'The Blurring Line between Freelance Journalists and Self-Employed Media Workers'.
33 Henkel et al., 'Do Online, Offline, and Multiplatform Journalists Differ...'
34 See, for example Davies and Simpson, 'BBC Presenter Taken off Air after "gleeful" Reaction'.
35 Hanitzsch and Vos, 'Journalistic Roles and the Struggle Over Institutional Identity'.

86 *A Profession Whose Time Has Come*

(such as sources), and of codes of ethics.[36] A comparison of those codes, in turn, suggests a common core of principles founded on what I described in Chapter 4 as journalism's definitive core mission of "fact-seeking and truth-telling."[37] But *standards*, against which conduct may be evaluated, require more specificity than the broad value statements with which many ethics codes have contented themselves. Standards also require regular reappraisal. To be fit for purpose in journalism today, a set of professional standards needs to illuminate often-opaque practices of presentation, emphasis, and automated curation.[38] Covering xenophobic movements may require guidance on balancing sensitivity to targeted groups against public-interest significance, and avoiding self-censorship given the likelihood of audience offence and disapproval.[39] Respecting privacy amid digital news' practically infinite availability suggests a need for standards of informed consent for sources and of *post hoc* updates or deletions.[40] The lightning-pace dissemination of anti-scientific theories can leave journalists hesitant to ask legitimate questions about public-health measures and preliminary studies; best-practice guidance can help reporters to avoid becoming mere stenographers for fallible experts.

Having myself led the revision of a national code of ethics, I know that compiling and regularly reviewing professional standards would be a tall order. But there's no reason to consider journalistic practice as innately more complex than other professions that manage these matters as a matter of course. News work is not, after all, brain surgery.

"Responsible" Journalism

One context in which journalists' professional standards are already parsed with rigour is in lawsuits for the tort most feared even by veteran journalists: defamation.

36 Harro-Loit, 'Journalists' Views about Accountability to Different Social Groups'; Ramaprasad et al., 'Ethical Considerations: Journalists' Perceptions of Professional Practice'.
37 Himelboim and Limor, 'Media Institutions, News Organizations, and the Journalistic Social Role Worldwide'.
38 Karlsson, Ferrer Conill, and Örnebring, 'Recoding Journalism'.
39 Perreault, *Digital Journalism and the Facilitation of Hate*.
40 Shapiro and Rogers, 'Who Owns the News?'; Schmidt, 'Unprepared for Unpublishing?'; Milosavljević, Poler, and Čeferin, 'In the Name of the Right to Be Forgotten'.

The perfect defence for libel in common law (but not all other legal systems) is to prove the truthfulness of the allegedly defamatory statement—which also happens to match the core purpose expected of all journalists. But judges in many places have come to understand that achieving judicial standards for proving factuality is sometimes an unreasonable ask for journalists in the real world, and may dismiss the libel action if the journalist has followed commonly accepted standards of reporting rigour and fairness. These duties of care may be specified in statutes or professional codes, but elsewhere have been recognized according to evidence of best practice in gathering, verifying, and presenting news.

Many common law jurisdictions, for example, offer a form of qualified-privilege libel defence that has become known as "responsible journalism." Local variations, whether enshrined in ongoing jurisprudence or in local statutes,[41] have been built upon a seminal British case in 1999 that produced what some lawyers call the *Reynolds* checklist.[42] It consists of a series of questions that, in my opinion, teachers of journalism in most places could usefully and easily adapt as rubrics for teaching professional standards for news reporting.

In an investigative reporting class, for instance, the slide projection might look something like this:

Responsible Journalism: Investigations

Is the alleged news a matter of public interest?
If someone's reputation is at stake, have they been given a reasonable chance to reply?
Does the story contain the gist of that person's side of the story?
Is the seriousness of the allegation matched by the reporter's verification rigour?
Are sources relaying their direct knowledge? Do they have an interest in perverting the truth?
Does the timing of reporting and publication match the urgency of the matter?
Does the tone and context match the degree of available certainty?

---

41 Barendt, 'Reynolds Revived and Replaced'.
42 Reynolds v. Times Newspapers Limited and Others, UKHL 45.

Positive answers to these questions would seem to translate readily as a list of duties for the category of investigative journalism, and fairly similar different duties can be derived for other categories. For curating commentary and opinion (the polar opposite of investigative journalism), the following might do, inspired by mixing *Reynolds* standards for truth-seeking with a separate libel defence for "fair comment"[43] and a splash of natural justice as per John Rawls.[44]

Responsible Journalism: Commentary and Analysis

Publish only opinions on matters of public interest.
Recognize the difference between a fact and an opinion.
Connect opinions with responsibly reported facts.
Broaden the range of perspectives to which audiences are exposed.
Purposefully include perspectives that challenge those who hold power.
Purposefully include perspectives likely to offend some audience members.[45]

These lists are, of course, merely illustrative, but the simplicity of building them suggests that professional standards aren't buried all that far from the surface where journalists consider themselves to be engaged in a public service. And if so, a stable marriage of press autonomy and meaningful accountability could, theoretically, be achieved.

Can this theory become practice? Norway's a good place to find out.

Embracing Accountability (A View From Norway)

"Church minister fired."[46]

The headline was straightforwardly factual, although the story underneath got a detail wrong. But that error was just the beginning

---

43 See, for example, WIC Radio Ltd. v. Simpson.
44 Hart, 'Rawls on Liberty and Its Priority'.
45 See Scrire, 'The New York Times' New Opinion Editor, Kathleen Kingsbury, on Reimagining Opinion Journalism'.
46 Lien, 'Kyrkjetenar har fått sparken'.

of what upset lay leaders in the church at Valle, upriver from Bygland. They complained to the Norwegian Press Council about the entire thrust of *Setesdølen*'s continuing coverage of a local dispute that had started with disagreement over locating a confirmation service during the Covid-19 pandemic.

As Sigurd Haugsgjerd's editorials made clear, he believed a veteran church worker had been unfairly punished for outspoken criticism of her employers. "They have frozen out enthusiastic and creative employees before," said one column. Repeated use of the term "church circus" [*kyrkjesirkus*] did little to assuage the umbrage.[47]

It may be relevant here that Haugsgjerd is an active Christian, a member of his own parish council who nevertheless prefers to walk the hills with his bird dogs on Sundays unless a newsworthy service gets him into his car with "fancy clothes" on, as he puts it. He has been quoted saying he doesn't fear dying, but wishes he could file a story about what happens afterward."[48] He told me he once said this to an archbishop: "I respect the Lord more than I respect his ambassadors."

But it's not just church authorities who have failed to get from Haugsgjerd the deference they might expect. He launched his journalistic career at the age of sixteen, with a report on local overfishing practices published in a Bergen paper. Lured inland to Setesdal's first newspaper in 1976, he built a reputation for plain speaking (or "not wrapping cotton in cotton," as he says) and taking on local political and business elites. *Setesdølen*'s front page once featured a picture of an incumbent mayor under the headline, "What has this man accomplished?" with clear implication of nothing. Another time, a group shot of a municipal committee ran under the headline, "The Judases" [*Judasane*], which he today thinks was overkill. When people threaten to cancel their subscriptions, Haugsgjerd directs them to the reception desk. A newspaper's job is not to take sides but to bring out "many voices," he says, but he does stand for "tolerance and diversity."[49]

Fellow journalists in the south now describe him as a "living legend,"[50] but that didn't get Haugsgjerd a free pass when the Valle parish council took the "church circus" coverage to the Norwegian

---

47 Homme, 'Setesdølen sitt vrengjebilde av kyrkja [Reader's letter]'.
48 Bjørkeli, 'Redaktøren som let språket synge'.
49 Kubens, 'Setesdølens Redaktør Bøyer Ikke Av for Verken Boikott Eller Press - Fvn.No'; Uleberg, 'Haugsgjerd Har Vore Bladstyrar i 39 År'.
50 Uleberg, 'Haugsgjerd Har Vore Bladstyrar i 39 År'.

Press Council. The adjudicating panel found nothing objectionable in editorial comments, but ruled the thread of news coverage "consistently tendentious." In particular, a news report that omitted mentioning that the parish council had been approached for comment was found to infringe Clause 4.14 of the national press ethics code, which states: "Dissemination of news must not be hampered by parties being unwilling to make comments or take part in the debate."[51]

As required by the Norwegian Press Association, to which all editors and publishers belong, the council's judgment was posted in full on *Setesdølen*'s website. But if editor Haugsgjerd was chastened by this, he chose an ironic way of showing it, running a news report about the hearing under the headline, "*Setesdølen*'s church circus toppled at Press Council."[52]

Press councils and ombudspersons adjudicate public complaints about journalists' conduct in many countries. If they rule in favour of a complainant, the offending news organization is required to publish the ruling. Generally, these bodies and their procedures are created unilaterally by a collective of news publishers for quite pragmatic reasons. As one internationally comparative study put it:

> A recognition of the importance of ethics and accountability, and debates between publishers and journalists, may be significant. However, the decisive trigger to the establishing, or reform, of a Press Council is commonly a proposal for statutory regulation that is held to threaten press freedom and results in a determined, pragmatic alternative response from the industry.[53]

Little is known about the impact of press-council rulings on continuing newsroom performance, careers, audience trust, or owners' profits, but theoretically, publishers in this scenario have struck a compromise, recognizing that journalists are bound by professional norms while maintaining authority over all other businesses' matters. When ownership consolidation led all but one

---

51 'Setesdølen braut god presseskikk'; 'Code of Ethics of the Norwegian Press'.
52 Haugsgjerd, 'Setesdølens kyrkjesirkus felt i PFU'.
53 Fielden, 'Regulating the Press: A Comparative Study of International Press Councils', 19.

of Canada's provincial press councils into untenable reliance on large media corporations' membership fees,[54] I was asked to lead a consultation that resulted in the creation of the first national news-media council.[55] Some journalists' eyes seemed glazed by the entire topic but most publishers welcomed the notion for two reasons. First, press councils provide people with complaints an alternative to lawsuits to state their case, thus saving publishers money. And second, voluntary accountability could help oppose political moves to imposed self-regulation, such as were then being promoted in Britain and Australia. The authors of those countries' proposals were accused of promoting something like (or, in the case of an Australian news executive, literally like) Stalinism.[56]

Norway's press council resides in a gabled three-storey building in downtown Oslo marked by an unobtrusive italic "*P*," for *Pressens hus* [Press House]. Its facilities are shared by what would, in many countries, comprise an unlikely collection of roommates most prominently including the Press Association and its constituent assemblies: the associations of editors and media owners, and the single national union that represents all journalists.

Posted on an upstairs hallway wall is a declaration of editorial autonomy, headed *Redaktorplakaten* and signed by the heads of the editors' and publishers' associations; its first version was agreed in 1953.[57] Around that time, a revision was being drafted for the nation's then-twenty-year-old code of press ethics; the new version began with a sober warning: "The printed word is a powerful weapon—abuse it not."[58] The code's current opening is, like the *Redaktorplakaten*, all about editorial autonomy. The press, it states, "cannot yield to any pressure from anybody who might want to prevent open debates, the free flow of information, free access to sources, and open debate on any matter of importance to society as a whole."[59]

---

54 The officially francophone province of Québec has a separate press council that is partially funded by the provincial government. See Shapiro, Taylor, and Tubb, 'Press Councils in Canada', 12.
55 See Watson, 'National Newsmedia Council Aims to Bring More Media into the Fold'.
56 Finkelstein and Tiffen, 'When Does Press Self-Regulation Work?', 964–65.
57 'Rights and duties of the editor'.
58 Bjerke, 'Samfunnsoppdraget—Fra Forpliktelse Til Rettighet'.
59 'Code of Ethics of the Norwegian Press', para. 1.3.

Even more unusually, editorial autonomy is enshrined in a Norwegian law that states:

> The publisher, owner or other company management cannot instruct or overrule the editor on editorial issues, nor can they demand to see print, text or pictures, or demand to hear or see programme material before it is made available to the public.[60]

The law specifically forbids any agreement to deviate from this stricture, "except to the advantage of the editor." If you, the reader, are sceptical about this working in practice, so was I, until I was pointed to cases where boards and individual owners who tried to put pressure on editors ended up backing down or leaving their positions.

But, yes, that's Norway.

Facing the Crisis of Trust

Earlier chapters have spotlighted a range of interconnected ways in which information disruption has challenged press freedom. These have included polarization of audience beliefs and expectations, declining revenues from advertising and subscription, disappearing news-media jobs, and audiences' declining interest in bare facts as compared with standpoint-aligned perceptions. All these realities pose critical threats to journalists' freedom to fulfil their core mission, and here is another: undisputed declines (in most countries) in the degree to which people expect news media to provide reliable information, especially online.

Once a year, the Reuters Institute asks digital news audiences in selected markets (forty-six countries in 2022) to what extent they agree with a range of statements about online news. The most basic statement is: "I trust most news most of the time." Most respondents in most countries *dis*agreed with this statement, with downward trends evident for several years. The world average trust level was 42 percent in 2022, and declining; below-average trust levels were reported for most countries in Asia, Latin America, and

---

[60] Act relating to the editorial independence and liability of editor-controlled journalistic media (The Media Liability Act) - Lovdata.

southern and eastern Europe plus the United Kingdom (34%) and the United States (26%, lowest of all). People in countries where news is trusted least are also most likely to say news is influenced by politics, business interests, or both.[61]

The lower levels of trust in news often mirror reduced trust in institutions, generally,[62] but the variations amongst media markets and amongst media brands may be more enlightening than the overall trend. News bosses in many countries might consider laying on counselling support ahead of the annual bear-market trendline updates for audience trust, but those near a North Sea beach—except for the British ones—might chill the bubbly, because healthy majorities in those countries continue to trust the news they see and hear.[63]

No one's yet tried a factor analysis against cold-water fish consumption, but correlations seem more likely with national wealth and education levels. The African survey data is still too limited (longitudinally and linguistically) to support transnational hypotheses, but the double-digit disparities amongst countries on all other continents may suggest that something more variable than digital disruption is implicated in the collapse of trust in news.

Supporting this impression are the significant differences in audience trust for individual media brands. A national aggregate showing overall distrust in "the media" (as people so often say) may easily veil successes that go against the tide. Public broadcasters, for example, exceed 80 percent trust scores in many democracies, as do some leading privately owned competitors. (One profound variation on this theme: the United States' most trusted news source in 2022 was the UK-based BBC News.)

Indicators of Reliability

Much may be learned from the reasons that some audience members give for continuing to trust the news they see and hear. Benjamin Toff and colleagues interviewed clusters of audience

61 Newman et al., 'Digital News Report 2022', 15–17.
62 Schiffrin, 'Credibility and Trust in Journalism'.
63 Belgium, Netherlands, Germany, Denmark, Norway, and Sweden, according to Newman et al., 'Digital News Report 2022' (the same is true of neighbouring Finland).

members in four representative countries and compared responses according to people's overall trust in news. Here are some things that "high-trust" interviewees claimed to consider in their news preferences: in-depth news coverage; impartiality about controversial topics; asking hard questions; a record of reliability over time; transparency about sources; correction of mistakes; and disclosure of conflict of interests.[64]

That's a surprisingly old-fashioned list to draw from a study fielded in the year 2021, and it's true that all attitudinal survey results deserve a pinch of people-say-the-darnedest-things scepticism. But then, one might turn from the high-trusters' list to the Reuters Institute's lists of most-trusted news brands and get beset by a nagging association with reputations for allegedly antiquated ideas—impartiality, depth, and so forth. And then, for yet more *deja-vu*, pin up lists of countries with high-trust scores, countries where people are most inclined to pay for digital news, and countries that comparative-media scholars have consistently affirmed as loci for strong pulls to "professional" autonomy rather than commercial and political loyalties. The moving finger writes all about, yes, professional standards.

Understandably, the many ways in which information landscapes have changed obviously and dramatically take up way more airtime than aspects that appear to show constancy. And the link between trust and perceived professionalism has hardly gone ignored. It has been hard not to notice the efforts of disrupted news brands to project an aura of professionalism, not all of which go demonstrably deeper than appearance. Publishers may establish a press council that's wholly dependent on publishers' support. Marketers may plaster buses with journalists' dressed-up photos and claims of expertise, reliability, and impartiality. Journalists may declare themselves autonomous even where publishers retain the power to fire them over content choices.

Some efforts along these lines aspire to something closer to peer review or standardization than to mere brand-marketing. One international project relies on demonstrated "trust indicators" to entitle news brands to display a "Trust Mark" logo.[65]

---

64 Toff et al., 'Listening to What Trust in News Means to Users', 11, 17–18; Fisher et al., 'Improving Trust in News', 1507–11.
65 'The Trust Project: FAQ'.

Another—spearheaded by Reporters Without Borders and backed by the European Commission—offers a standardized process for evaluating editorial processes and autonomy, with a suggestion that the resulting reports can be used by funders, advertisers and regulators as, in effect, certificates of quality.[66]

With time, perhaps, a degree of consensus may distinguish genuine attempts at accountability from rhetoric and half-measures. The Reuters Institute's corpus of trust studies seems to suggest that evidence of professionalism in news content may be more influential on audiences than brand-marketing efforts—that, in effect, audiences might be harder to fool than some publishers would like to think. It's worth recalling the old saying: "Never trust a man who says, 'Trust me'."

A Question of Will

Robust professionalism in news media—the real thing, not the semblance—means owners ceding autonomy to editors, editors recognizing journalists' quality concerns as labour rights, and all regular editorial contributors being emboldened by job security. It also involves journalists accepting accountability to peers' judgement; those averse to joining professional associations may need to get over themselves. Unions accustomed to compete amongst themselves may need to learn to collaborate. Perhaps the hardest ask of all, for unlovable journalists, is to build habits of critically reflecting on their own methods and assumptions—which, without formal accountability, requires unusual force of will.

When right-wing populists won electoral gains in the United States in 2016 and Germany in 2020 by impugning the reliability of elites including news media, some journalists shifted into attack mode, fiercely playing up voters' biases and alleged lack of education or rebelling against journalistic norms regarding newsworthiness or the right of reply. Others looked inward, examining the extent to which bias and selectivity had, perhaps, helped lower everyone's expectations of journalists' role performance. The former response is psychologically understandable, but

---

66 'About Us: Journalism Trust Initiative (JTI)'.

professional discipline favours the latter. As a German study of post-election opinion columns concluded:

> The criticism raised by right-wing populists and others or the doubts arising within journalism seem to be sufficiently relevant to justify a metajournalistic debate. Professionalism seems to be the legitimate and/or effective answer. Rather than deconstructing the norms or the criticism, journalists are admonished to follow them more strictly—a metajournalistic discourse that is, maybe a bit unexpectedly, directed inwardly, even in the general press, but may also contribute to legitimizing journalistic practices in the eyes of a larger public.[67]

Given the big differences between well-grounded systems of professional accountability and more free-wheeling efforts to enhance news-brand reputations, the hardest question is, do news people have sufficient will to replace the latter with the former? It doesn't seem likely, or, at least, easy.

At *Pressens hus*, I met Elin Floberghagen, a former journalists' union leader who is now secretary general of the Norwegian Press Association. I asked her how it was possible that journalists, editors and media owners could have agreed on effective self-regulation of professional news media work, evidently without surrendering their various principles, their competing interests, or the trust of their shared audiences.

Her answer: "We talked for a hundred years." I believed her—this was Norway, after all, and she was speaking about a journey of collaboration that began with agreement on her country's first national press code, literally a century ago.

Will the globally disrupted press be allowed a hundred years to tackle disputes over its freedom? Once again, it seems neither likely nor easy, but perhaps we may allow ourselves one more chapter to examine some options.

---

67 Krämer and Langmann, 'Professionalism as a Response to Right-Wing Populism?'

6 The Precarious Future of a Disrupted Press

Abstract

This final chapter draws together the multidimensional threats that face journalistic autonomy as news media move beyond the initial period of digital disruption. The challenges differ markedly from nation to nation, even where other democratic indicators are in place. The government of India, for example, is bound by a liberal constitution but has brutally suppressed journalism in the territory of Kashmir. In some situations, journalism is a life-threatening activity. Elsewhere, critical problems with revenue and credibility threaten the quality and value of journalistic effort. A precarious future is assured for journalism almost everywhere in the absence of radical departures from the pre-disruption assumptions of publishers, front-line journalists, and editors. The book ends with a list of potential strategies for defending the press by embracing the necessity of systemic change.

The Day They Switched Off Journalism

In the early hours of Monday, August 5th, 2019, Adil Amin Akhoon woke up to a text message asking if his internet was working. It was, but not for much longer than it took to read a report in *The Hindu* confirming that the government of India had imposed a curfew on the state of Jammu & Kashmir (J&K)—and then, there was nothing.[1]

---

1 Adil Amin Akhoon was interviewed in Hindi by Rajalaxmi Nayak, a student of professional communication and news studies at Toronto Metropolitan

DOI: 10.4324/9781003223146-6

Akhoon and other Kashmiris had sensed something big was coming—there were more soldiers on the streets than usual, and 4G mobile data had begun disappearing on Sunday. By noon next day, broadband internet, cable TV, and even landline phones were cut. Only when all communication with Kashmir was one-way from outside did the real news come from the parliament in Delhi: the government of prime minister Narendra Modi was abrogating Article 370—the constitutional disposition that had, since 1954, provided semi-autonomous status for J&K as India's only Muslim-majority state. By nightfall, it was done: the laws of the Union of India would now apply throughout the state.[2]

The government said a communications blackout was needed to avoid violent protests. It took a few weeks for landline phones to be restored, five months for low-data mobile services. 4G was gone until January, 2021—a world-record shutdown of seventeen months.[3] For Akhoon, a freelance journalist based in Srinagar, the disconnection went way beyond inconvenience. "All Kashmir was a prison," he said three years later. "It was the biggest prison."

Perhaps that was the idea. Locking up journalists would have been more trouble for the authorities; the blackout silenced them, and everyone else, with much less fuss.

Freedom of the press is not mentioned explicitly in India's constitution but the union's supreme court ruled in 1984 that it's "included" in the guarantee of free expression.[4] This has not deterred what Reporters Without Borders (RSF) has described as "violence against journalists, the politically partisan media and the concentration of media ownership" that places press freedom "in crisis."[5]

If so, India is not alone. The word *crisis* gets overused—by journalists amongst others—but the forces threatening autonomous journalism around the world are now many and serious

---

University. She conducted both bibliographic and interview research for this chapter.

2 'Kashmir Updates: Rajya Sabha Passes Bill'; ANI (Asian News International), 'Constitution (Application to Jammu and Kashmir) Order 2019 (C.O. 272)'; 'Kashmir: India Top Court Orders Review'.
3 Ehsan, '17 Months on, 4G Internet Services Restored in Jammu and Kashmir'.
4 Indian Express Newspapers (Bombay) Private Ltd. v. Union of India at III (p. 19).
5 'India (RSF)'.

enough to support strong language and justify unprecedented countermeasures. These various obstacles have been described separately in previous chapters, but let's pause here to assimilate their combined breadth and depth.

First, people do still shoot messengers. The number of journalists killed while (or for) doing their jobs averaged nearly a hundred a year between 2016 and 2020. Just 13 percent of such cases had been "judicially resolved" in the past fifteen years, according to UNESCO. At time of writing in late 2022, the RSF press freedom barometer showed five hundred journalists currently in prison worldwide, with the rate of journalists' killings running at more than one per week. Journalists whose work troubles governments, businesses, organized crime, or populist groups have seen their radio stations shuttered in Nigeria and received credible death threats in Italy, have been physically assaulted in the United States and targeted by police in Brazil, and on, and on, and on.[6] Whether disruption has affected journalists' physical safety is unclear—journalism has never been a safe way to earn a living, especially for those covering wars, tyranny, and uprisings. But online threats, abuse, and harassment of journalists—especially women journalists and members of other marginalized groups—leaves them beset by well-grounded fear for their lives and the well-being of their families.[7]

Second, the overall state of public information is unsound. Disinformation abounds while reliable news gets scarcer and harder to recognize. Today's government-size dominators of information markets are widely expected to moderate user-generated content but there's no broad consensus on purposes or methods, with actual governments requiring highly varied approached to deleting or restoring content.[8] Likewise, conventional news media struggle to focus curatorial criteria and editing standards for controversial opinions, humour, and content that touches marginalized groups.[9]

---

6 'RSF Press Freedom Index, 2022'; 'World: Abuses in Real Time (RSF)'.
7 Benequista, *Journalism Is a Public Good*, 11.
8 See, for example: 'German Court Faults Facebook's Past Handling of Hate Speech'; Collins, 'France Gives Social Media 1 Hour to Delete the Worst Illegal Content'; Amarasingam, 'Thread by @AmarAmarasingam'; Hannan, 'Facebook Banned My Perfectly Harmless Article—and I Think I Know Why'; Hallam, 'Twitter Just Caved To Modi'.
9 Hern, 'Facebook Guidelines Allow Users to Call for Death of Public Figures'; Klonick, 'Inside the Making of Facebook's Supreme Court'.

Human moderation of user-generated content is slow, expensive, and highly subjective while artificial-intelligence tools are designed to analyze and respond to existing interests and habits (is the user a churchgoer or a women's health worker?) rather than broaden their knowledge. These tools are calculated to amplify or hide content without considering complex factors such as context, purpose, and news value.[10]

The third besetting obstacle to press freedom is the decayed state almost everywhere of trust and responsibility, on which press freedom is grounded, as economic challenges continue to weaken both the quantity and the quality of journalism. Audiences have found enough alternative and free sources of information to crush revenue streams needed to support the costs of newsgathering and editing. Impoverished news outlets have shrunken and closed. Concentration of ownership has compromised choice and range of journalistic coverage. Resources have shrunk for editorial leadership, mentorship, verification, and corrections. Editorial autonomy has been compromised by the increased urgency of business objectives (such as audience engagement and speed) compared with core ethical obligations (such as accuracy and fairness).

This dystopian picture is as far as can be imagined from a world served well by a free press—that is, one untouched by interference and censorship, enabled by protections for autonomy and newsgathering, and held accountable for professional practices.[11]

To illustrate the difference that could be made in real life by the presence or absence of press freedom's enabling factors, may I offer a parable? If you judge its essence plausible, it may clarify what's at stake. Let's call it:

The Short Happy Life of Somewhere Today

Your home town of Somewhereville, population 10,000, currently has a single provider of local news: the weekly *Somewhereville Gazette*, with a local staff of three. Editing and production happen at the

---

10 Maréchal and Biddle, 'It's the Business Model:', 5,22.
11 Benequista, *Journalism Is a Public Good*, 23.

headquarters of the *Gazette*'s owners, Everywhere Media Inc (EMI) in faraway Gotham City; EMI also runs dozens of local outlets, talk radio stations, plus a national casino chain.

So, one Wednesday night after a recreational soccer game, you and the j-school-educated goalie and the treasurer/coach/manager (who staffed the production booth at the community radio station until it closed) drink a few beverages and sketch up a few napkins. A few creative and well-hydrated Wednesdays later, the first edition of a newsletter, *Somewhere Today*, is launched, based right there in the clubhouse. Help arrives from a high school journalism club and a bright intern paid through a grant from the goalie's partner's mom, an investment banker. Weirdly, perhaps, *Today* is soon doing a demonstrably better job of keeping folk informed than the sad old *Gazette*. You're selling enough subscriptions and used-car ads to buy and stock a second-hand refrigerator for the clubhouse/newsroom.

One Wednesday, you find an unaddressed brown envelope taped to the beverage cooler; inside is a bank statement and a few other sheets full of numbers and dates. The intern makes a few calls, checks some documents down at Town Hall, and *Today*'s next edition features your first screaming headline:

CORRUPTION IN MAYOR'S OFFICE? THOUSANDS MISSING

The mayor sues, of course. You can't produce your evidence without exposing your confidential source. "It's basic journalism ethics," you tell the court, and the judge (who golfed with the mayor just last week) bursts out laughing. It turns out *Today* doesn't qualify for the privilege of protecting sources because under your country's laws, you have to be a member of a press council to claim it, and the membership fee is somewhat higher than your beverage bill.

So you settle with the mayor and run a grovelling correction. The intern quits. The town council decides preferred seating for its meetings and access to documents is for press-council members only. The police won't let you anywhere near a fiery student protest at the local college, because they don't think you're objective (you supported the students' cause in an editorial last week). Finally, the clubhouse's electric supply gets shut off by order of the municipal safety inspector. What's left of *Today*'s newsroom manages to empty the cooler before it fully thaws, and then ceremonially buries all remaining napkins under a penalty spot before calling it a wrap. Before heading home, you adjust the scoreboard to read: POWER 1, PEOPLE 0.

If your town, city or country has substantially better access to news than Somewhereville's, it likely enjoys either some aspects of UNESCO's "enabling environment" for press freedom or the services of journalists who still believe in the *idea* of journalism—its purpose, its norms, its worth, and its future.

Journalists like this exist in real life—lots of them. We've met a few in this book, and we're not quite done.

News under the Guns (A View from Kashmir)

One of Adil Amin Akhoon's most memorable assignments in the University of Kashmir's master's program in journalism was to interview a dead man's widow and son. Afzal Guru had been executed in 2013 for his role in a deadly attack on the Indian parliament. Listening to family memories of a man considered a terrorist by some while others believed him framed,[12] Akhoon realized this was work he wanted to go on doing.

Born and raised in the Kashmir valley, beneath the Himalayas, he grew up swimming in crystal-blue mountain streams and lakes, but in the shadow of an ever-expected India-Pakistan war over the state's territory. A young Adil and his friends were heading to grade-school one day when teargas exploded nearby; down the street, protesters were pelting security forces with stones. When he learned to read, he'd scan the newspaper for local safety hazards

---

12 Roy, 'The Hanging of Afzal Guru Is a Stain on India's Democracy'.

or for an explanation of why school was shut: "Is it a curfew? Is it a strike? Was another militant shot in the city? That's how my first interactions with news were," he says.

A few years later, his uncle, who had some connections to local politicians, was abducted and murdered. The family learned about this, too, from the newspaper: "That this has happened," Akhoon recalls, "a man with these identification marks. This body has been found and this police station can be contacted. We went there; we saw his clothes and we identified him. I was very young."

He says he went freelance by choice after finishing a disillusioning newsroom internship arranged through the j-school. Akhoon wanted to look at all sides of a story, pick it apart and then put it together with care; his editor just wanted him to file. So, in 2019, he co-founded an online magazine, *Mountain Ink*, with a group of friends.[13] It offers a mix of narrative journalism, photo features, quirky short items, and news updates. Most of it is far from political, but in J&K, hazards are everywhere. A video interview with a fisher included a comment about the unavailability of local fish—the only fish were from outside, and the result was a polluted Kashmir.

Could a political metaphor be read in this? Yes, it could, as was made clear by a non-optional visit to a police station. "Have I not warned you about this?" Akhoon reminded a younger colleague afterward. "We are on the radar now. We have eyes on us."

When the Internet shutdown ended,[14] Akhoon wrote a story for Al Jazeera about the workarounds Kashmiri journalists had found to get the news out.[15] But politics doesn't seem his chief interest; he'd just as soon take a horseback journey to see a spring-cleaning festival in an isolated mountain village, share a meal with villagers, and chat about their fruit trees. For the *South China Morning Post*, he profiled a village that has fought domestic violence by forbidding dowries.[16] For the US-based *New Lines Magazine,* he interviewed women who had been weaving carpets since childhood, plying a

---

13 'Mountain Ink; Home'.
14 Ehsan, '17 Months on, 4G Internet Services Restored in Jammu and Kashmir'.
15 Akhoon and Parvaiz, 'How Do Journalists Work under Information Blockades?'
16 Akhoon, 'The Kashmir Village That Ended Domestic Violence by Banning Dowries'.

now-vanishing craft brought to the valley by Persian artisans in the 1400s.[17] "There are tourists who come in and marvel at the beauty of this place," he says. "But what lies beyond the beauty of this place... you'll find in the stories of Kashmiri people."

Yet, there is no getting away from his homeland's troubles. "Documenting this time in Kashmir is my duty," he says. "After ten or twenty years there will be Kashmiris or even people from outside who might want to read about the information blockade, about what really happened when Article 370 was revoked."

Financial instability isn't fun, but it's the cost of freelancing, Akhoon says. "I have enough faith in my ideas," he says, to keep going when story pitches are rejected. As for leaving the field, his *zameer* [Urdu for conscience] wouldn't allow it. "It's like that thing..., you know, when you take an oath, or a promise. You can't go back."

Renewing the Freedom of a Precarious Press

It matters, of course, how governments treat the troublesome presence of news media, and with what degree of brutality. But the shape of press freedom's future doesn't depend *only* or *primarily* on the goodwill of politicians. The first of many excursions taken in this book dropped in on the dawn of news media in Africa and closed with the following reflection:

> As with Junius's printers, so also with the [*South African Commercial*] *Advertiser* and parallel battles that publishers (not journalists) fought one by one in those early days, press freedom advanced mainly through someone trying to shoot it down, and the target demanding justice.

Battles fought? Shooting? Demanding? To hear some news-media owners in prosperous democracies describe their strategies today, one might think politicians are genial uncles who can be relied upon, just because they're good people, to help news media out with legislated financial subsidies or tax relief or laws that force news intermediaries (a.k.a. Meta and Google) to share advertising

---

17 Amin, Ali, and Farooq, 'The Unraveling of Kashmir's Handmade Carpet Industry'.

revenue on news. (See Chapter 3) These moves might conceivably help to irrigate some local news deserts, but at the price of at least an apparent conflict of interest for journalists. This point doesn't necessarily contradict the policy case for supporting the press any more than is true for public broadcasting resources or, for that matter, the funding of any public benefit. Taxpayers foot the bill for road engineering and ambulance services, so why not the gathering of news? No reason why not, a thoughtful taxpayer might respond: just so long as journalists—like engineers and paramedics—are held accountable for adherence to professional standards.

Right, that. Meaningful undergirding of professionalism seems the first and most obvious of several steps that could be taken to strengthen press freedom, where they haven't been taken already (see Chapter 5). Obvious, and yet not even close to being accepted in places where, well, it's not customary. And so here, at the end of our journey, we find the key to resolving many disputes over the freedoms of a disrupted press. It is the looming, urgent need for publishers and journalists to choose between what has been customary and what is called for.

Looming, urgent, and yet somehow, in many places, not even on the radar.

You've seen the movie, surely. An eccentric, annoying, and unfashionably bespectacled oceanographer, biochemist, or astronomer warns of an approaching killer wave, virus, or asteroid, but no one believes it. The government is preoccupied with a coming election, as is the generic version of CNN. The army is busy doing what armies do. Everyone else is shopping, picking the kids up, and having sex (not simultaneously). Cue the CGI. For a grisly half hour or more, people drown, burn, shrivel, scream, hug, weep, die. Some save themselves by good luck or ingenuity. The most highly paid member of the cast—the one most likely to front a sequel—saves many and then falls in love (bad eyewear notwithstanding), pens a best-seller, and lives happily, if not ever after, then at least until The End.

If you're still reading this, you're likely one of those who've already noticed how large the free-press-killing asteroid looms. Maybe the realization came when people started shooting visibly "other" people because they believed widely circulated reports (perhaps oft-repeated on a major TV "news" network) about an officially sponsored program to "ethnically replace" their own kind.[18] Maybe you don't live in that particular country, but you can easily find closer-to-home signs that people have lost the capacity to find and believe information about what's actually going on. (See Chapter 4.)

Where enough challenges of this magnitude confront any given news system, it's hard for anyone to make informed choices that touch on public affairs. This is not a news-business crisis; it's a *freedom* crisis, and the biggest question becomes: how many people in any given place actually care enough about their diminishing freedom to do something about it?

There's no way to answer this question, but those who *do* care will surely, at some point, eschew bemoaning the disrupted past and start making the kind of radical choices (not incremental repairs and rhetorical leaps) required to break the siege on the disrupted press's freedoms. The logic of preceding chapters suggests unprecedented combinations of brave and focused action by publishers and journalists will be required. The following ideas are offered, not as a manifesto, but merely as examples of approaches that may be seen (in some places, not all) as dramatic changes, but ones perhaps worth a think-about.

> ***Publicly Guarantee Editorial Autonomy***: Since everyone seems to agree that newsroom autonomy is core to press freedom, it seems reasonable to expect publishers to guarantee it in writing—together with a muscular means of arbitrating potential disputes with the editors they hire.
>
> ***Actively Combat Polarization***: The Russian journalist and Nobel laureate Dmitry Muratov has said one purpose of journalism is to "make people into allies."[19] This is not as touchy-feely a call as it may sound. Information disorder presents journalists with a seldom-comfortable responsibility to provide people with access to unexpected facts and diverse perspectives that they don't get in their polarized channels. If a news outlet can't dare to shock its audience members with surprising facts and unwelcome opinions, why should they respect it?

---

18 Confessore and Yourish, 'Replacement Theory, a Fringe Belief'.
19 Sackur, 'Maria Ressa and Dmitry Muratov' at 0:17;49 .

Provide "Valuable" Journalism: A public-good publisher seeks to understand the communities they serve—which is a more complex endeavour than following data aggregates. Dutch researchers Irene Costera Meijer and Hildebrand P. Bijleveld suggested that news content is "valuable" to news consumers to the extent that it draws on, and respectfully complements, people's own perspectives and experience with a range of information that they consider important and useful.[20] Respecting news consumers includes taking a serious and open-minded interest in communities well beyond publishers' and editors' own circles, and maybe taking stock of who's been over-served and underserved to date.[21] That would improve the public-service case, as does noticing the diversity of people's experience, attitudes and interests, following these and reflecting them in newsroom composition.

Raise the Bar for News Choices: As Guy Berger has written, journalists have a clear responsibility to confront the rise of "fake news" head-on and:

> tack more closely to professional standards and ethics, to eschew the publishing of unchecked information, and to take a distance from information which may interest some of the public but which is not in the public interest.[22]

Embrace Professional Standards: As disruption proceeds, positive protections for newsgathering will continue to be claimed by a widening set of self-avowed journalists with only two possible endings: privileges for everybody and therefore nobody, or tightened professional boundaries. Courts and legislatures have been known to go in either direction, but when they do recognize journalistic privileges, there's often a link with accountability for ethical standards. The European Court of Human Rights, for instance, has held that journalists' right to divulge otherwise protected information on issues of general interest is conditional on "acting in good faith and on an accurate factual basis and that they

---

20 Costera Meijer and Bijleveld, 'Valuable Journalism'.
21 Edmonds, 'Editors Agree'.
22 Berger, 'Foreword', 9.

provide 'reliable and precise' information in accordance with the ethics of journalism."[23] A similar contingency is built into South African data-protection law, which specifically defers to safeguards built into codes of journalistic ethics.[24]

Strengthen Accountability: In many parts of the world, press councils depend on major news organizations to make payroll and lack the power to suspend or expel even the worst repeat offenders, which limits their options about whom to accept as members in the first place. Systemic stability is a forgotten essential in accountability structures, which are themselves essential to journalists' professionalism.[25] As Louis Hodges pointed out:

> Basic morality dictates that individuals (or organizations) are accountable to all those whose lives and well-being are significantly affected by the professional's conduct. In our professional lives we owe an accounting to those stakeholders for whom our professional performance has significance.[26]

Accept Self-regulation as the Price of Professional Privileges: News media in some parts of the world see meaningful self-regulation as a corollary to autonomy (see Chapter 5) or as a bulwark against politically driven restrictions.[27] This does not mean it should be legally required—freedom of expression allows everyone the same right to publish anything legal. It's just inevitably going to get harder for independent all-comers to claim the legal exemptions (positive rights) for newsgathering.

But I must be honest: the journey I've shared with you in this book leaves me realizing I simply don't understand why so many Anglo-American journalists continue to resist professional self-regulation so deeply. Journalists are not, after

---

23 Hovlid, 'Finding a Judicial Definition of Journalism: A Challenging Exercise in the Digital Age', 219.
24 Protection of Personal Information Act, chap. 2, s. 7 (1)-(2).
25 Shapiro, 'Toward an International Perspective on Media Accountability'.
26 Newton, Hodges, and Keith, 'Accountability in the Professions: Accountability in Journalism', 173, 186.
27 Masuku, 'Total Media Self-Regulation in Africa Still to Be Achieved'; Plessing, 'Shifting the South African Media Diversity Debate'.

all, mere messengers, as some like to say; what they choose to inquire into, or to ignore, can bring governments down, turn ordinary folk into heroes, make businesses bankrupt, give people hope, and break their hearts. Trust-averse audiences may be forgiven for wondering why people with such power resist having to explain themselves to their peers.

Embrace Collective Responsibility: I have often noticed and heard of successful journalists ignoring the bullying and harassment of younger or less empowered colleagues. Professionalism means, in part, both earning and expecting collective respect, and standing together with vulnerable colleagues such as rookies, interns, those with short-term contracts, and freelancers. And where employers endanger journalists' autonomy rather than defending it, there's a solution that, according to Nicole Cohen and Greig de Peuter, has been especially effective in all-digital news environments: urgent, determined unionization.[28]

Let Editors Lead: I have heard enough reporters talk about their bosses to know that journalists direct loyalty and respect to those editors who stand up for newsrooms' autonomy and for audiences' right to be told the uncompromising truth. These editors expect publishers to steer clear of influencing news content. They expect beat reporters to beat bushes rather than symbiotically schmooze with sources, accepting performative answers to predictable questions.[29] They expect news desks to treat press releases as potential ideas, not prewritten copy. And they respect audiences too much to tolerate lazy thinking about news choices.[30]

Take Less-travelled Roads: It costs money and time to get stuff right, to correct errors, and to engage with the people who might rely on what's published.[31] A quality newsroom needs mid-level editorial leadership plus consistent professional development. Affording these increasingly threatened expenditures requires hard choices based on priorities rather than habits. Source pickup footage for the next royal wedding

---

28 Cohen and de Peuter, *New Media Unions*, xviii.
29 van Dalen, Albæk, and de Vreese, 'Suspicious Minds', 158–59; Brants et al., 'The Real Spiral of Cynicism?', 36–37.
30 Harcup and O'Neill, 'What Is News?'
31 Zahay et al., 'The Labor of Building Trust'.

instead of going the full on-the-spot Monty. Report others' election polls and cancel your own. Fire that high-priced columnist with loyal readers but predictable viewpoints.

Keep Analytics in Their Place: Paying attention to the economic seduction of analytics spikes isn't optional but it's dangerous when it stands opposed to original, rigorous, and significant truth-finding. Nicole Blanchett has shown how editors and producers face pressure to deliver high traffic to news posts, moment by moment. Without a culture of respect for the news itself, this pressure can squeeze out stories of greater social value. Some journalists even come to feel they must choose between their careers and their ideals.[32] An editorial culture that values journalism for its substance and integrity not only provides journalists with a sense of purpose, it also makes possible a reduction in audience scepticism.

Learn Humility: This is hard, and not only because journalistic work requires high self-confidence. But a touch of evident professional humility can't harm the trust problem. You and I might find a know-it-all quite entertaining or quite the opposite, but we'd both hesitate to loan them a car. When a reporter starts telling me what a president is thinking tonight, I start thinking about bed. Opinion writers, too, might be encouraged to reflect regularly on the delta between who they think they are and who their readers think they are.[33]

Lean on Peers: Journalists could learn something from hospital physicians in cultivating a habit of private, honest discussions about unexpected case outcomes. The aim of such conversations should be to improve future work through building a shared sense of quality and integrity[34] or, in Jane Singer's words, a "framework for distinguishing between high-quality information that is a service to the public and low-quality information that may be a disservice."[35]

Be Cautious and Transparent with Government Dealings: There's nothing wrong with expecting taxpayers to support public

---

32 Blanchett, 'Participative Gatekeeping', 785–86.
33 Taibbi and Medina, 'The New York Times Editorial Board's Creepy Avengers Fantasy'.
34 Anderson, Downie, and Schudson, *The News Media*, 62.
35 Singer, 'Journalism and Digital Technologies', 214–15.

services, but secret negotiations between news media and governments are no way to promote citizens' trust in the press. Also, government promises are innately temporary: if the current head of government isn't a blatant enemy of fact-oriented independent newsgathering, the next one could be. Budget priorities change; legislation can be repealed. News media need more stable bridges to their future than politics can provide.

Form Global Alliances against Disinformation: Much journalism, however local in origins, has a potentially global audience plus global liabilities, and is disseminated for profit by intermediary platforms owned by global corporations such as Google and Meta. Yet, quests for fair financial compensation from platforms have, until this time of writing, all been geographically local to a publisher or group of publishers, sometimes coordinated nationally or required by national laws.

Marcelo Rech, former news director of the RBS news group in southern Brazil and former president of the World Editors Forum, has a different idea: an internationally brokered convention against disinformation, signed by a wide range of stakeholders in media systems "in the same manner that we are joining different stakeholders for a global agreement about climate change." Commitments to self-regulation—and not just by journalists—would need to be part of the outcome. The biggest "polluters" of global information should "pay for the clean-up," Rech told me, and he believes Big Tech will do so to the extent that it provides significant corporate benefit. A predictable global system of compensation, with clarity on expectations and eligibility, would be one such benefit, and would allow news media greater security than any other option on the current landscape.[36]

What's Worth Fighting For

History may see the thriving, profitable, comfortable press that existed in many parts of the world between Hiroshima and 9/11

---

36 See Rech, 'Brazil's Riots Highlight the Need for a Global Antidote to Disinformation'.

not as a template but as an interruption of news media's natural precarity. We may learn to look back on that period nostalgically, as one might a cool dry week in the tropics, and on disruptions to journalism's comfort as the monsoon season's rain. We got drenched yesterday and again this afternoon, as we will tomorrow, and, well, we're going to need a bigger umbrella. Many news media people (myself included, for too long) rested on nice-day-isn't-it assumptions until belatedly noticing foundations rotting and cracks in the walls.

In the rotting-house situation, many a homeowner might sell up and move on. Fortunately, despite the dramatic challenges presented by disruption, journalists are not giving up their collective vocation *en masse*. Their work goes on; their passion endures.

In the forty-eight hours before I wrote the sentence you're now reading, I learned the following about matters of public interest thanks to the reporting of professional journalists around the world:

> Stray bullets from a military shooting range prevent children in the Nigerian state of Oyo from going to school.[37]
>
> Indonesia's parliament has moved to make sex outside marriage a crime punished by imprisonment of up to a year.[38]
>
> A U.K. legislator earned twenty-nine million pounds for recommending a company to supply protective equipment during the Covid-19 pandemic.[39]
>
> The outgoing government of Jair Bolsonaro blocked, released, and then again blocked the release of all funds due to universities in Brazil.[40]
>
> A hair salon in the city of Thanh Hoa, Vietnam, sends teams out on motorcycles to outdoor gathering places, where they set out plastic chairs and provide free haircuts to poor people—first come, first served.[41]

37 Abelade, 'Living in the Shadow of Death'.
38 Mackintosh, 'Indonesia Set to Punish Sex before Marriage with Jail Time'.
39 Conn, 'The Yacht, the Wedding and £29m'.
40 Cuenca, 'Governo volta atrás e zera caixa de universidades e institutos federais'.
41 Lê Hoàng, 'Salon Tóc Di Động Dành Cho Người Nghèo'.

Canada has seen an increase in medically assisted suicides chosen by people with disabilities who could not find affordable solutions for care.[42]

To help heal lasting resentments since the second world war, a rural community in Australia that once housed an internment camp now co-sponsors a student exchange with a Japanese high school. [43]

A city in the United States banishes those convicted of petty crimes from entire neighbourhoods.[44]

Authors of books formerly banned in Philippines continue to speak out against censorship despite a change of government.[45]

People who work in heavy labour and later develop chronic conditions may have trouble getting unemployment, disability, and insurance benefits in Germany.[46]

I now know these ten things, and so do you, because ten or more journalists did their jobs. This is what people in many places stand to lose unless new ways get found to keep reliable news flowing.

The disputes are tormenting, the disruption severe. The lights are going out for the free press and switching them back on will be hard. But that's what freedom is: hard.

---

42 Cribb, Buckley, and Gribilas, 'Why Michael Chose Assisted Death over a Life of Pain and Poverty'.
43 Midori, 'Japanese, Australian Students Bond Where Their Countries Once Fought'.
44 Kohler, 'St. Louis Can Banish People From Entire Neighborhoods'.
45 Bermeo, '"Subversive" Authors Continue to Fight after Voided Ban on Their Books'.
46 Neth, 'Spendenaktion Hilfe Für Den Nachbarn'.

References

Abelade, Lukman. 'Living in the Shadow of Death: Ibadan Communities Where Children Boycott School to Avoid Soldiers' Bullets'. *The Punch*, 13 November 2022. https://punchng.com/living-in-the-shadow-of-death-ibadan-communities-where-children-boycott-school-to-avoid-soldiers-bullets/.

Abernathy, Penelope Muse. 'News Deserts and Ghost Newspapers: Will Local News Survive?' Chapel Hill, North Carolina: Center for Innovation and Sustainability in Local Media Hussman School of Journalism and Media, 2020.

'About Us: Journalism Trust Initiative (JTI)'. Accessed 4 February 2023. www.journalismtrustinitiative.org/about.

Act relating to the editorial independence and liability of editor-controlled journalistic media (The Media Liability Act)—Lovdata, Norwegian Media Authority § (2020). https://lovdata.no/dokument/NLE/lov/2020-05-29-59.

Adam, G. Stuart. 'Notes Towards a Definition of Journalism: Understanding an Old Craft as an Art Form'. In *Journalism: The Democratic Craft*, edited by G. Stuart Adam and Roy Peter Clark, 344–70. New York: Oxford University Press, 2006.

Africa Check, Chequeado, and Full Fact. 'Fact Checking Doesn't Work (the Way You Think It Does)'. *Full Fact*, 20 June 2019. https://fullfact.org/blog/2019/jun/how-fact-checking-works/.

Aird, Michael J., Ullrich K. H. Ecker, Briony Swire, Adam J. Berinsky, and Stephan Lewandowsky. 'Does Truth Matter to Voters? The Effects of Correcting Political Misinformation in an Australian Sample'. *Royal Society Open Science* 5, no. 12 (December 2018): 180593. https://doi.org/10.1098/rsos.180593.

Akhoon, Adil. 'The Kashmir Village That Ended Domestic Violence by Banning Dowries'. *South China Morning Post*, 21 August 2021, sec.

This Week in Asia. www.scmp.com/week-asia/people/article/3145676/kashmir-village-put-end-domestic-violence-banning-dowries.

Akhoon, Adil, and Saliq Parvaiz. 'How Do Journalists Work under Information Blockades?' *Al Jazeera*, 7 July 2022. https://institute.aljazeera.net/en/ajr/article/1933.

Alexander, Larry. *Is There a Right of Freedom of Expression?* Cambridge: Cambridge University Press, 2005.

Amado, Adriana, and Silvio Waisbord. 'Divided We Stand: Blurred Boundaries in Argentine Journalism'. In *Boundaries of Journalism: Professionalism, Practices and Participation*, edited by Matt Carlson and Seth C. Lewis, 51–66. *Explorations in Communication and History*. London; New York: Routledge, Taylor & Francis Group, 2015.

Amarasingam, Amarnath. 'Thread by @AmarAmarasingam'. *Twitter/Threadreader*, 10 January 2022. https://threadreaderapp.com/thread/1348147867739975681.html.

Amazeen, Michelle A., Chris J. Vargo, and Toby Hopp. 'Reinforcing Attitudes in a Gatewatching News Era: Individual-Level Antecedents to Sharing Fact-Checks on Social Media'. *Communication Monographs* 86, no. 1 (2019): 112–32. https://doi.org/10.1080/03637751.2018.1521984.

Amin, Adil, Sharafat Ali, and Bisma Farooq. 'The Unraveling of Kashmir's Handmade Carpet Industry'. *New Lines Magazine*, 19 May 2021. https://newlinesmag.com/reportage/the-unraveling-of-kashmirs-handmade-carpet-industry/.

Anderson, C. W. *Rebuilding the News: Metropolitan Journalism in the Digital Age*. Philadelphia: Temple University Press, 2013.

Anderson, C. W., Leonard Downie, and Michael Schudson. *The News Media: What Everyone Needs to Know*. New York, NY: Oxford University Press, 2016.

Anderson, Elizabeth. 'Feminist Epistemology and Philosophy of Science'. In *The Stanford Encyclopedia of Philosophy*, edited by Edward N. Zalta, Spring 2020. Metaphysics Research Lab, Stanford University, 2020. https://plato.stanford.edu/archives/spr2020/entries/feminism-epistemology/.

ANI (Asian News International). 'Constitution (Application to Jammu and Kashmir) Order 2019 (C.O. 272)'. *Tweet. Twitter*, 5 August 2019. https://twitter.com/ANI/status/1158255571155525637.

Anonymous. *The Letters of Junius*. Wikisource, n.d. https://en.wikisource.org/wiki/Letters_of_Junius.

Barbier, Frédéric. *Gutenberg's Europe: The Book and the Invention of Western Modernity*. Oxford: Polity Press, 2016.

Bardi, Anat, and Shalom H. Schwartz. 'Values and Behavior: Strength and Structure of Relations'. *Personality and Social Psychology Bulletin*

29, no. 10 (1 October 2003): 1207–20. https://doi.org/10.1177/0146167203254602.
Barendt, Eric. *Freedom of Speech*. 2nd ed. Oxford University Press, 2007. https://doi.org/10.1093/acprof:oso/9780199225811.001.0001.
———. 'Reynolds Revived and Replaced'. *Journal of Media Law* 9, no. 1 (2 January 2017): 1–13. https://doi.org/10.1080/17577632.2017.1315900.
Barnoy, Aviv, and Zvi Reich. 'The When, Why, How and So-What of Verifications'. *Journalism Studies* 20, no. 16 (10 December 2019): 2312–30. https://doi.org/10.1080/1461670X.2019.1593881.
Bastiat, Frédéric. 'The Law (Chapter 2)'. In *Selected Essays on Political Economy*. Irvington-on-Hudson, NY: The Foundation for Economic Education, Inc. Accessed 21 November 2021. www.econlib.org/library/Bastiat/basEss2.html.
Bechtold, Eliza. 'Free Speech in America: Is the US Approach Fit for Purpose in the Age of Social Media?' The Conversation, 8 January 2021. http://theconversation.com/free-speech-in-america-is-the-us-approach-fit-for-purpose-in-the-age-of-social-media-152854.
Bell, Emily, and Taylor Owen. 'The Platform Press: How Silicon Valley Reengineered Journalism'. *Columbia Journalism Review*, 29 March 2017. www.cjr.org/tow_center_reports/platform-press-how-silicon-valley-reengineered-journalism.php.
Bellingcat Investigation Team. 'The Making of QAnon: A Crowdsourced Conspiracy'. *Bellingcat*, 7 January 2021. www.bellingcat.com/news/americas/2021/01/07/the-making-of-qanon-a-crowdsourced-conspiracy/.
Benequista, Nicholas, ed. *Journalism Is a Public Good: World Trends in Freedom of Expression and Media Development; Global Report 2021/2022*. UNESCO Digital Library. Accessed 8 September 2022. https://unesdoc.unesco.org/ark:/48223/pf0000380618?2=null&queryId=0a30ee11-7640-48c0-b1c3-8d7e1e5dc867.
Bentham, Jeremy. 'Anarchical Fallacies'. *Headline Series*, no. 318 (Winter 1998): 56.
Benton, Joshua. 'This Report Sees Journalistic "Bias" Less as Partisanship and More as Relying on Too-Comfortable Habits'. *Nieman Journalism Lab*, 30 January 2023. www.niemanlab.org/2023/01/this-report-sees-journalistic-bias-less-as-partisanship-and-more-as-relying-on-too-comfortable-habits/.
Berger, Guy. 'Foreword'. In *Journalism, 'Fake News' and Disinformation: A Handbook for Journalism Education and Training*, edited by Cherilyn Ireton and Julie Posetti. Paris: UNESCO, 2018. https://en.unesco.org/fightfakenews.
———. 'Problematizing Race for Journalists: Critical Reflections on the South African Human Rights Commission Inquiry into Media Racism'. *Race, Gender & Class* 11, no. 2 (30 April 2004): 11.

Berlin, Isaiah. 'Two Concepts of Liberty'. In *Liberty*, by Isaiah Berlin, 166–217. edited by Henry Hardy, 2nd ed. Oxford University Press, 2002. https://doi.org/10.1093/019924989X.003.0004.

Bermeo, Farley, Jr. '"Subversive" Authors Continue to Fight after Voided Ban on Their Books'. *Rappler*, 1 December 2022, sec. Life and Style. www.rappler.com/life-and-style/literature/authors-continue-fight-after-voided-ban-books/.

Bernier, Marc-François. 'Understanding Journalisms: From Information to Entertainment by Persuasion and Promotion'. *Canadian Journal of Communication*, 27 September 2022, e20220033. https://doi.org/10.3138/cjc.2022.0033.

'Bhisho Massacre Memorial This Thursday'. *Grocott's Mail*, 6 October 2017.

Binnie, Ian, and Antonin Scalia. 'The Charter at 25 (Debate)'. *CPAC*, 16 February 2007. www.cpac.ca/episode?id=af6ece2f-bda8-457b-9257-83b8a725511a.

Bird, Wendell. *The Revolution in Freedoms of Press and Speech: From Blackstone to the First Amendment and Fox's Libel Act*. Oxford: Oxford University Press, 2020.

Bjerke, Paul. 'Samfunnsoppdraget—Fra Forpliktelse Til Rettighet'. In *Journalistikkens Samfunnsoppdrag*, edited by Sigurd Allern and Johann Roppen. Kristiansand (Norway): IJ-forlk, 2010.

Bjørkeli, Johs. 'Redaktøren som let språket synge'. *Faerelandsvennen*. 7 June 2013, sec. Lokalt. www.fvn.no/nyheter/lokalt/i/6eEnz/redaktoeren-som-let-spraaket-synge.

'Black Wednesday, the Banning of 19 Black Consciousness Movement Organisations'. *South African History Online*. Accessed 14 February 2022. www.sahistory.org.za/dated-event/black-wednesday-banning-19-black-consciousness-movement-organisations.

Blanchett, Nicole. 'Participative Gatekeeping: The Intersection of News, Audience Data, Newsworkers, and Economics'. *Digital Journalism* 9, no. 6 (25 January 2021): 773–91. https://doi.org/10.1080/21670811.2020.1869053.

Bogart, Leo. 'Reflections on Content Quality in Newspapers'. *Newspaper Research Journal* 25, no. 1 (Winter 2004): 40–53.

Borchers, Callum. 'Media Standards on Lies and False Statements Are Changing Fast'. *Washington Post*, 3 January 2017. www.washingtonpost.com/news/the-fix/wp/2017/01/03/media-standards-on-lies-and-false-statements-are-changing-fast/.

Bourdieu, Pierre. 'The Political Field, the Social Science Field, and the Journalistic Field'. In *Bourdieu and the Journalistic Field*, edited by Benson, Rodney and Erik Neveu, 1–28. Cambridge: Polity, 2005.

Boyd, Heather. 'Accreditation and Access in a Changing Media Landscape: A Cross-Jurisdictional Analysis of Accreditation of

Canadian Legislative Reporters and an Examination of the Issue of Media Access'. *Government of Alberta,* 17 March 2016.

Bracken, Amber. 'About Me'. Amber Bracken Documentary Photographer. Accessed 22 August 2022. www.amberbracken.com/about.

———. 'Kamloops Residential School'. *World Press Photo of the Year,* 19 June 2021. www.worldpressphoto.org/contest/2022.

Brants, Kees, Claes de Vreese, Judith Möller, and Philip van Praag. 'The Real Spiral of Cynicism? Symbiosis and Mistrust between Politicians and Journalists'. *The International Journal of Press/Politics* 15, no. 1 (1 January 2010): 25–40. https://doi.org/10.1177/1940161209351005.

Brooke, Heather. *The Revolution Will Be Digitised: Dispatches from the Information War.* London: William Heinemann, 2011.

Callison, Candis, and Mary Lynn Young. 'Attending to The Reckoning and the Voiceless: Multiple Truths, Systems Approaches to Journalism'. In *Handbook of Global Media Ethics,* edited by Stephen J.A. Ward, 1223–31. Cham: Springer International Publishing, 2021. https://doi.org/10.1007/978-3-319-32103-5_61.

Calvo, Ernesto, Natalia Aruguete, Tiago Ventura, Adrián Contursi, and Katherine Miller. 'Chequeado in Argentina: Fact-Checking and the Spread of Disinformation on Social Media'. The Interdisciplinary Laboratory of Computational Social Science, University of Maryland, February 2021. https://chequeado.com/wp-content/uploads/2021/02/Chequeado-in-Argentina.-Fact-checking-and-the-spread-of-disinformation-on-social-media.pdf.

Cameron, Jamie. 'Freedom of Expression and the Charter: 1982-2022 (Part 1 of 5)'. *Centre for Free Expression,* 10 February 2022. https://cfe.ryerson.ca/blog/2022/02/freedom-expression-and-charter-1982-2022-part-1-5.

———. 'Section 2(b)'s Other Fundamental Freedom: The Press Guarantee, 1982-2012'. *Comparative Research in Law & Political Economy,* 1 January 2013. https://digitalcommons.osgoode.yorku.ca/clpe/270.

Canada Election 2021: English-Language Federal Leaders' Debate | FULL. Global News, 2021. www.youtube.com/watch?v=Tr_CwDsQzg8.

'Canadian Charter of Rights and Freedoms'. *Constitution Act,* 1982. 7 August 2020. https://laws-lois.justice.gc.ca/eng/Const/page-12.html.

Carey, James W. 'Why and How: The Dark Continent of American Journalism'. In *Reading the News,* edited by Robert Karl Manoff and Michael Schudson, 146–96. New York: Pantheon Books, 1987.

Carlson, Matt. 'Boundary Work'. In *The International Encyclopedia of Journalism Studies,* 1–6. John Wiley & Sons, Ltd, 2018. https://doi.org/10.1002/9781118841570.iejs0035.

References

Cecco, Leyland. 'Canada: Outcry after Video Shows Hospital Staff Taunting Dying Indigenous Woman'. *The Guardian*, 30 September 2020. www.theguardian.com/world/2020/sep/30/joyce-echaquan-canada-indigenous-woman-hospital.

Chase, Anthony. 'The Transnational Muslim World, Human Rights, and the Rights of Women and Sexual Minorities'. *Muslim World Journal of Human Rights* 4, no. 1 (2007): i–14.

Chasi, Colin. 'Ubuntu and Freedom of Expression'. *Ethics & Behavior* 24, no. 6 (2 November 2014): 495–509. https://doi.org/10.1080/10508422.2014.894913.

Chen, Yen-Pin, Yi-Ying Chen, Kai-Chou Yang, Feipei Lai, Chien-Hua Huang, Yun-Nung Chen, and Yi-Chin Tu. 'The Prevalence and Impact of Fake News on COVID-19 Vaccination in Taiwan: Retrospective Study of Digital Media'. *Journal of Medical Internet Research* 24, no. 4 (26 April 2022): e36830. https://doi.org/10.2196/36830.

Chequeado. 'Los Juegos de Chequeado [The Chequeado Games]'. *YouTube*, 1 November 2017. www.youtube.com/watch?v=VQbMe8XjQDs.

Christensen, Clayton M., David Skok, and James Allworth. 'Breaking News: Mastering the Art of Disruptive Innovation in Journalism'. *Nieman Reports*, 15 September 2012. https://niemanreports.org/articles/breaking-news/.

Christians, Clifford G., Shakuntala Rao, Stephen J. A. Ward, and Herman Wasserman. 'Toward a Global Media Ethics: Theoretical Perspectives'. *Ecquid Novi: African Journalism Studies* 29, no. 2 (January 2008): 135–72. https://doi.org/10.1080/02560054.2008.9653382.

Cinelli, Matteo, Gianmarco De Francisci Morales, Alessandro Galeazzi, Walter Quattrociocchi, and Michele Starnini. 'The Echo Chamber Effect on Social Media'. *Proceedings of the National Academy of Sciences* 118, no. 9 (2 March 2021): e2023301118. https://doi.org/10.1073/pnas.2023301118.

'Coastal GasLink Drops Charges against Journalists Arrested by RCMP during Enforcement of Pipeline Injunction', *CBC News*, 22 November 2021. www.cbc.ca/news/canada/british-columbia/amber-bracken-journalist-released-1.6258584.

Coddington, Mark. '"Glory and Honor": How Professional Identity Shapes the Way Journalists Do Their Work'. *Nieman Lab* (blog), September 2019. www.niemanlab.org/2019/09/glory-and-honor-how-professional-identity-shapes-the-way-journalists-do-their-work/.

'Code of Ethics of the Norwegian Press'. *Presse.no.*, 1 January 2021. https://presse.no/pfu/etiske-regler/vaer-varsom-plakaten/vvpl-engelsk/.

Coester, Dana. 'A Matter of Space: Designing Newsrooms for New Digital Practice'. *American Press Institute*, 18 October 2017. www.americanpressinstitute.org/publications/reports/strategy-studies/matter-of-space/.

Cohen, Nicole S. 'At Work in the Digital Newsroom'. *Digital Journalism* 7, no. 5 (28 May 2019): 571–91. https://doi.org/10.1080/21670 811.2017.1419821.

———. 'Cultural Work as a Site of Struggle: Freelancers and Exploitation'. *TripleC* 10, no. 2 (2012): 141–55. https://doi.org/10.31269/triplec. v10i2.384.

Cohen, Nicole S., and Greig de Peuter. *New Media Unions: Organizing Digital Journalists*. Milton, UK: Taylor & Francis Group, 2020.

Collins, Katie. 'France Gives Social Media 1 Hour to Delete the Worst Illegal Content'. *CNET*, 14 May 2020. www.cnet.com/tech/mobile/fra nce-gives-social-media-companies-one-hour-to-delete-illegal-content/.

Conboy, Martin. 'Journalism History'. In *The Handbook of Journalism Studies*, edited by Karin Wahl-Jorgensen and Thomas Hanitzsch, 2nd edition. International Communication Association (ICA) Handbook Series. New York, NY: Routledge, 2019.

Confessore, Nicholas, and Karen Yourish. 'Replacement Theory, a Fringe Belief Fueled Online, Is Refashioned by G.O.P.', 15 May 2022. www. nytimes.com/2022/05/15/us/replacement-theory-shooting-tucker-carl son.html?referringSource=articleShare.

Conn, David. 'The Yacht, the Wedding and £29m: Michelle Mone's Life during the Covid Crisis'. *The Guardian*, 23 November 2022, sec. UK news. www.theguardian.com/uk-news/2022/nov/23/the-yacht-the-wedd ing-and-29m-michelle-mones-life-during-the-covid-crisis.

'Constitution of the Republic of South Africa', 1996. South African Government. www.gov.za/documents/constitution-republic-south-africa-1996.

Convention on the Elimination of All Forms of Discrimination against Women, United Nations § (1979). www.ohchr.org/en/instruments-mec hanisms/instruments/convention-elimination-all-forms-discrimination-against-women.

Copeland, David A., and Daniel Schorr. *The Idea of a Free Press: The Enlightenment and Its Unruly Legacy*. Evanston, Ill: Northwestern University Press, 2006.

Costera Meijer, Irene, and Hildebrand P. Bijleveld. 'Valuable Journalism'. *Journalism Studies* 17, no. 7 (2 October 2016): 827–39. https://doi.org/ 10.1080/1461670X.2016.1175963.

Cowan, Geoffrey, and David Westphal. 'Public Policy and Funding the News'. Center on Communication Leadership & Policy, USC Annenberg School for Communication & Journalism, January 2010. https://fundingthenews.usc.edu/report/.

Craft, Stephanie. 'Distinguishing Features: Reconsidering the Link Between Journalism's Professional Status and Ethics—Stephanie Craft, 2017'. *Journalism & Communication Monographs* 19, no. 4

(2017): 260–301. https://journals.sagepub.com/doi/abs/10.1177/1522637917734213.

Cribb, Robert, Charlie Buckley, and Thea Gribilas. 'Why Michael Chose Assisted Death over a Life of Pain and Poverty'. *Toronto Star*, 10 November 2022. www.thestar.com/2022/assisted-death.html.

Cuenca, Paola. 'Governo volta atrás e zera caixa de universidades e institutos federais'. *SBT News*, 2 December 2022, sec. educação. www.sbtnews.com.br/noticia/educacao/232285-governo-volta-atras-e-zera-caixa-de-universidades-e-institutos-federais.

Das, Ronnie, and Wasim Ahmed. 'Rethinking Fake News: Disinformation and Ideology during the Time of COVID-19 Global Pandemic'. *IIM Kozhikode Society & Management Review* 11, no. 1 (1 January 2022): 146–59. https://doi.org/10.1177/22779752211027382.

'Database of Global Fact Checking Sites'. Reporters Lab. Accessed 6 October 2012. https://reporterslab.org/fact-checking/.

Davies, Gareth, and Craig Simpson. 'BBC Presenter Taken off Air after "gleeful" Reaction to Boris Johnson Pulling out of Tory Leadership Race'. *The Telegraph*, 24 October 2022. www.telegraph.co.uk/news/2022/10/24/watch-bbc-presenter-admits-gleeful-reaction-tory-leadership/?WT.mc_id=e_DM52955&WT.tsrc=email&etype=Edi_FPM_New&utmsource=email&utm_medium=Edi_FPM_New20221024&utm_campaign=DM52955.

'Declaration of the Rights of Man—1789'. Avalon Project (Yale Law School). Accessed 23 February 2022. https://avalon.law.yale.edu/18th_century/rightsof.asp.

'Declaration of Windhoek on Promoting an Independent and Pluralistic African Press'. UNESCO, 1991. https://unesdoc.unesco.org/ark:/48223/pf0000090759?posInSet=2&queryId=3aebea3e-fcd3-4925-8e14-af9b9f4ec10d.

'Declarations, Reservations, Objections and Notifications of Withdrawal of Reservations Relating to the Convention on the Elimination of All Forms of Discrimination against Women', 10 April 2006. United Nations. https://documents-dds-ny.un.org/doc/UNDOC/GEN/N06/309/97/PDF/N0630997.pdf?OpenElement.

de Peuter, Greig. 'Creative Economy and Labor Precarity: A Contested Convergence'. Edited by Jack Z. Bratich. *The Journal of Communication Inquiry* 35, no. 4 (2011): 417–25. https://doi.org/10.1177/0196859911416362.

de Staël, Germaine. *Considérations Sur Les Principaux Événemens de La Révolution Française, Ouvrage Posthume*. 2nd ed. Vol. 1. Paris: Delaunay, 1818. https://oll.libertyfund.org/title/l-considerations-sur-les-principaux-evenemens-de-la-revolution-francaise-3-vols.

de Villiers, James. 'Stefaans Brümmer, AmaBhungane Co-Founder, on Crooks, Graft and Why He's Moving on'. *News24*. Accessed 10 February 2022. www.news24.com/news24/analysis/saturday-profile-the-man-behind-guptaleaks-and-arms-deal-exposes-and-why-hes-moving-on-20210821.

Deuze, Mark. 'What Is Journalism?: Professional Identity and Ideology of Journalists Reconsidered'. *Journalism* 6, no. 4 (2005): 442–64.

Dickson, Annabelle. 'Britain Tries to Work out What a Journalist Is'. *Politico Europe*, 26 August 2021. www.politico.eu/article/britain-asks-who-is-journalist-define/.

'Dispatch from the Front Lines: There's No Non-Political Way to Decide Who's a Journalist'. Substack newsletter. *The Line (blog)*, 9 April 2022. https://theline.substack.com/p/dispatch-from-the-front-lines-theres.

Donsbach, Wolfgang. 'Psychology of News Decisions: Factors behind Journalists' Professional Behavior'. *Journalism* 5, no. 2 (1 May 2004): 131–57. https://doi.org/10.1177/146488490452002.

Dragomir, Marius. *Reporting Facts: Free from Fear or Favour*. World Trends in Freedom of Expression and Media Development. Paris: UNESCO, 2020. https://unesdoc.unesco.org/ark:/48223/pf0000375061.

Du Plessis, Tim. 'Newspaper Management Keeps Quiet About Its Role in Apartheid: In the Afrikaans Press, Some Reporters Decide to Testify'. *Nieman Reports* 52, no. 4 (Winter 1998). https://web.archive.org/web/20060908021708/http://www.nieman.harvard.edu/reports/98-4NRwint98/DuPlessis.html.

Edmonds, Rick. 'Editors Agree: Journalism Is Increasingly Super-Serving Richer and More Educated Audiences and Leaving Others Behind'. *Poynter*, 11 January 2022. www.poynter.org/ethics-trust/2022/editors-agree-journalism-is-increasingly-super-serving-richer-and-more-educated-audiences-and-leaving-others-behind/.

Edwards, David. *Guardians of Power: The Myth of the Liberal Media*. Ann Arbor, MI: Pluto, 2006.

Ehsan, Mir. '17 Months on, 4G Internet Services Restored in Jammu and Kashmir'. *Hindustan Times*, 6 February 2021. www.hindustantimes.com/india-news/17-months-on-4g-internet-services-restored-in-jammu-and-kashmir-101612564917419.html.

Eldridge, Scott A. 'Boundary Maintenance and Interloper Media Reaction'. *Journalism Studies* 15, no. 1 (2 January 2014): 1–16. https://doi.org/10.1080/1461670X.2013.791077.

European Convention on Human Rights (2021). www.echr.coe.int/documents/convention_eng.pdf.

Fairbank, Viviane. 'How Do We Exit the Post-Truth Era? Why Fact-Checking Alone Won't Save Us from Fake News'. *The Walrus*, 7 April 2021. https://thewalrus.ca/how-do-we-exit-the-post-truth-era/.

Feather, Norman T. 'Values, Valences, and Choice: The Influence of Values on the Perceived Attractiveness and Choice of Alternatives'. *Journal of Personality and Social Psychology; Washington* 68, no. 6 (June 1995): 1135.

Feather, Norman T. 'Values, Valences, and Course Enrollment: Testing the Role of Personal Values within an Expectancy-Valence Framework'. *Journal of Educational Psychology* 80, no. 3 (1988): 381–91. https://doi.org/10.1037/0022-0663.80.3.381.

Fielden, Lara. 'Regulating the Press: A Comparative Study of International Press Councils'. *Reuters Institute for the Study of Journalism*, April 2012. https://reutersinstitute.politics.ox.ac.uk/sites/default/files/2017-11/Regulating%20the%20Press.pdf.

Finkelstein, Ray, and Rodney Tiffen. 'When Does Press Self-Regulation Work?' *Melbourne University Law Review* 38, no. 3 (2015): 944–67. https://doi.org/10.3316/informit.291330636037688.

Fisher, Caroline, Terry Flew, Sora Park, Jee Young Lee, and Uwe Dulleck. 'Improving Trust in News: Audience Solutions'. *Journalism Practice* 15, no. 10 (26 November 2021): 1497–515. https://doi.org/10.1080/17512786.2020.1787859.

Flaxman, Seth, Sharad Goel, and Justin M. Rao. 'Filter Bubbles, Echo Chambers, and Online News Consumption'. *Public Opinion Quarterly* 80, no. S1 (2016): 298–320. https://doi.org/10.1093/poq/nfw006.

Fleerackers, Alice, Michelle Riedlinger, Laura Moorhead, Rukhsana Ahmed, and Juan Pablo Alperin. 'Communicating Scientific Uncertainty in an Age of COVID-19: An Investigation into the Use of Preprints by Digital Media Outlets'. *Health Communication*, 3 January 2021, 1–13. https://doi.org/10.1080/10410236.2020.1864892.

Frankenberg, Günter. 'Human Rights and the Belief in a Just World'. *International Journal of Constitutional Law* 12, no. 1 (1 January 2014): 35–60. https://doi.org/10.1093/icon/mot068.

'The Trust Project: FAQ'. Accessed 17 June 2022. https://thetrustproject.org/faq/.

Galan, Lucas, Jordan Osserman, Tim Parker, and Matt Taylor. 'How Young People Consume News and the Implications for Mainstream Media'. *Flamingo/Reuters Institute for the Study of Journalism*, 29 August 2019. https://apo.org.au/node/256781.

Gallagher, Margaret. 'Gender Inequality, Media and Development'. In *Media Matters: Perspectives on Advancing Governance & Development from the Global Forum for Media Development*, edited by Mark Harvey. Internews Europe, 2007. https://internews.org/wp-content/uploads/legacy/resources/mediamatters.pdf.

Galpaz-Feller, Pnina. 'David and the Messenger—Different Ends, Similar Means in 2 Samuel 1'. *Vetus Testamentum* 59, no. 2 (2009): 199–210.

'GDP per Capita (Current US$) | Data'. The World Bank. Accessed 25 November 2022. https://data.worldbank.org/indicator/NY.GDP.PCAP.CD.

General Regulation under the Security from Trespass and Protecting Food Security Act, S.O. 2020, c.9, Ontario § (2020). www.ontario.ca/laws/regulation/200701.

'German Court Faults Facebook's Past Handling of Hate Speech'. *AP News*, 29 July 2021. https://apnews.com/article/technology-europe-business-courts-migration-4d6dedb19d44df371465528d097c5872.

Gershberg, Zachary, and Sean D. Illing. *The Paradox of Democracy: Free Speech, Open Media, and Perilous Persuasion*. Chicago: University of Chicago Press, 2022.

Gillers, Stephen. *Journalism under Fire: Protecting the Future of Investigative Reporting*. New York: Columbia University Press, 2018.

Giménez, José. 'Martín Guzmán: "El 94% de las posiciones [arancelarias] hoy tiene una alícuota menor que cuando empezamos el gobierno"'. *Chequeado (blog)*, 6 May 2022. https://chequeado.com/ultimas-noticias/guzman-el-94-de-las-posiciones-arancelarias-hoy-tiene-una-alicuota-menor-que-cuando-empezamos-el-gobierno/.

Glendon, Mary Ann. 'The Forgotten Crucible: The Latin American Influence on the Universal Human Rights Idea'. *Harvard Human Rights Journal* 16 (2003): 27–40.

Goodale, Mark, ed. *Letters to the Contrary: A Curated History of the UNESCO Human Rights Survey. Stanford Studies in Human Rights*. Stanford, California: Stanford University Press, 2018.

———. 'The Myth of Universality: The UNESCO "Philosophers' Committee" and the Making of Human Rights'. *Law & Social Inquiry* 43, no. 3 (2018): 596–617. https://doi.org/10.1111/lsi.12343.

Granger, Jacob. 'New Powers for UK Media to Report on Family Courts'. *Journalism.Co.Uk (blog)*, 30 January 2023. www.journalism.co.uk/news/the-new-powers-for-uk-media-to-report-on-family-courts/s2/a1004966/.

Graves, Lucas. 'Boundaries Not Drawn: Mapping the Institutional Roots of the Global Fact-Checking Movement'. *Journalism Studies* 19, no. 5 (4 April 2018): 613–31. https://doi.org/10.1080/1461670X.2016.1196602.

Greenspon, Edward. 'The Shattered Mirror: News, Democracy and Trust in the Digital Age | Public Policy Forum', 2 February 2017. https://shatteredmirror.ca/download-report/.

Haidt, Jonathan, and Greg Lukianoff. 'The Polarization Spiral'. *Persuasion (blog)*, 17 August 2022. www.persuasion.community/p/the-polarization-spiral?utm_medium=email.

Hallam, Luke. 'Twitter Just Caved To Modi'. *Persuasion (blog)*, 30 January 2023. www.persuasion.community/p/twitter-just-caved-to-modi?utm_medium=email.

References

Hallin, Daniel C., and Paolo Mancini. *Comparing Media Systems: Three Models of Media and Politics*. New York: Cambridge University Press, 2004.

Hamada, Basyouni, Sallie Hughes, Thomas Hanitzsch, James Hollings, Corinna Lauerer, Jesús Arroyave, Verica Rupar, and Sergio Splendore. 'Editorial Autonomy: Journalists' Perceptions of Their Freedom'. In *Worlds of Journalism: Comparing Journalistic Cultures across the Globe.*, edited by Thomas Hanitzsch, Folker Hanusch, Jyotika Ramaprasad, and Arnold S. De Beer. New York: Columbia University Press, 2019.

Hanitzsch, Thomas, and Tim P. Vos. 'Journalistic Roles and the Struggle Over Institutional Identity: The Discursive Constitution of Journalism'. *Communication Theory (1050-3293)* 27, no. 2 (May 2017): 115–35. https://doi.org/10.1111/comt.12112.

Hanitzsch, Thomas, Tim Vos, Olivier Standaert, Folker Hanusch, Jan Fredrik Hovden, Liesbeth Hermans, and Jyotika Ramaprasad. 'Journalists' Views on Their Place in Society'. In *Worlds of Journalism: Comparing Journalistic Cultures across the Globe.*, edited by Thomas Hanitzsch, Folker Hanusch, Jyotika Ramaprasad, and Arnold S. De Beer. New York: Columbia University Press, 2019.

Hannan, Daniel. 'Facebook Banned My Perfectly Harmless Article—and I Think I Know Why'. *The Telegraph*, 28 February 2021. www.telegraph.co.uk/news/2021/02/28/facebook-banned-perfectly-harmless-article-think-know/.

Hanusch, Folker, and Thomas Hanitzsch. 'Comparing Journalistic Cultures Across Nations'. *Journalism Studies* 18, no. 5 (2017): 525–35. https://doi.org/10.1080/1461670X.2017.1280229.

Hanusch, Folker, and Kim Löhmann. 'Dimensions of Peripherality in Journalism: A Typology for Studying New Actors in the Journalistic Field'. *Digital Journalism*, 13 December 2022, 1–19. https://doi.org/10.1080/21670811.2022.2148549.

'Happiness, Benevolence, and Trust During COVID-19 and Beyond'. Accessed 25 November 2022. https://worldhappiness.report/ed/2022/happiness-benevolence-and-trust-during-covid-19-and-beyond/.

Harber, Anton. 'How to Ensure Media Is Not a Pawn for Politicians'. *Business Day.* 20 October 2020, sec. Life.

———. *So, for the Record: Behind the Headlines in an Era of State Capture*. Jeppestown, South Africa: Jonathan Ball Publishers, 2020.

———. *Southern African Muckraking: 300 Years of Investigative Journalism That Has Shaped the Region*. Auckland Park, South Africa: Jacana, 2018.

Harcup, Tony, and Deirdre O'Neill. 'What Is News?' *Journalism Studies* 18, no. 12 (2 December 2017): 1470–88. https://doi.org/10.1080/1461670X.2016.1150193.

Hardimon, Michael O. 'Role Obligations'. *The Journal of Philosophy* 91, no. 7 (1 July 1994): 333–63. https://doi.org/10.2307/2940934.

Hardin, Marie, and Andrew C. Billings. 'A Fracturing Profession on Shifting Terrain: Challenges and Directions for Sports Journalism'. *Communication & Sport* 10, no. 3 (1 June 2022): 395–97. https://doi.org/10.1177/21674795221095618.

Hardt, Michael, and Antonio Negri. *Commonwealth*. First Harvard University Press paperback edition. Cambridge, Mass London: Belknap Press of Harvard University Press, 2011.

Harro-Loit, Halliki. 'Journalists' Views about Accountability to Different Social Groups'. *Journal of Media Ethics* 30, no. 1 (2015): 31–43. https://doi.org/10.1080/08900523.2014.985296.

Hart, H. L. A. 'Rawls on Liberty and Its Priority'. *The University of Chicago Law Review* 40, no. 3 (1973): 534–55. https://doi.org/10.2307/1599247.

Hatcher, John, and Emily Haavik. '"We Write with Our Hearts"'. *Journalism Practice* 8, no. 2 (4 March 2014): 149–63. https://doi.org/10.1080/17512786.2013.859828.

Haugsgjerd, Sigurd. 'Setesdølens kyrkjesirkus felt i PFU'. *Setesdølen*, 26 January 2022. www.setesdolen.no/nytt/setesdolens-kyrkjesirkus-felt-i-pfu/.

Headley, John M. *The Europeanization of the World: On the Origins of Human Rights and Democracy*. Princeton: Princeton University Press, 2016.

Henkel, Imke, Neil Thurman, Judith Möller, and Damian Trilling. 'Do Online, Offline, and Multiplatform Journalists Differ in Their Professional Principles and Practices? Findings from a Multinational Study'. *Journalism Studies* 21, no. 10 (26 July 2020): 1363–83. https://doi.org/10.1080/1461670X.2020.1749111.

Herman, Edward S., and Noam Chomsky. *Manufacturing Consent: The Political Economy of the Mass Media*. New York: Pantheon Books, 1988.

Hermida, Alfred. 'Tweets and Truth: Journalism as a Discipline of Collaborative Verification'. *Journalism Practice* 6, no. 5–6 (1 October 2012): 659–68. https://doi.org/10.1080/17512786.2012.667269.

Hern, Alex. 'Facebook Guidelines Allow Users to Call for Death of Public Figures'. *The Guardian*, 23 March 2021. www.theguardian.com/technology/2021/mar/23/facebook-guidelines-allow-for-users-to-call-for-death-of-public-figures.

Himelboim, Itai, and Yehiel Limor. 'Media Institutions, News Organizations, and the Journalistic Social Role Worldwide: A Cross-National and Cross-Organizational Study of Codes of Ethics'. *Mass Communication and Society* 14, no. 1 (30 December 2010): 71–92. https://doi.org/10.1080/15205430903359719.

Homme, Lisbeth D. 'Setesdølen sitt vrengjebilde av kyrkja [Reader's letter]'. *Setesdølen,* 13 June 2021. www.setesdolen.no/meiningar/set esdolen-sitt-vrengjebilde-av-kyrkja/.

Hovlid, Ellen Lexerød. 'Finding a Judicial Definition of Journalism: A Challenging Exercise in the Digital Age'. In *Human Rights, Digital Society and the Law: A Research Companion,* edited by Mart Susi, 209–24. Routledge Research in Human Rights Law. London; New York, NY: Routledge/Taylor & Francis Group, 2019.

Hugo Bustios Saavedra v. Peru, Case 10.548, Report N° 38/97 (Inter-Am. C. H. R. 16 October 1997).

Hujanen, Jaana, Juho Ruotsalainen, Viljami Vaarala, Katja Lehtisaari, and Mikko Grönlund. 'Performing Journalism. Making Sense of Ethical Practice within Local Interloper Media'. *Journalism,* 4 October 2022, 146488492211316. https://doi.org/10.1177/1464884922 1131626.

Ichou, Rachel Pollack, ed. *World Trends in Freedom of Expression and Media Development: Special Digital Focus 2015.* World Trends in Freedom of Expression and Media Development. Paris: UNESCO Publishing, 2015.

'Independent Advisory Board on Eligibility for Journalism Tax Measures—Annual Report 2020-2021'. Canada Revenue Agency, 22 June 2021. www.canada.ca/en/revenue-agency/services/tax/businesses/ topics/corporations/business-tax-credits/qualified-canadian-journal ism-organization/independent-advisory-board-on-eligibility-for-jou rnalism-tax-measures-annual-report-2020-2021.html.

'India | RSF'. Reporters Without Borders. Accessed 16 November 2022. https://rsf.org/en/country/india.

Indian Express Newspapers (Bombay) Private Ltd. v. *Union of India* (Supreme Court of India 6 December 1984).

'International Covenant on Civil and Political Rights'. OHCHR. Accessed 6 September 2022. www.ohchr.org/en/instruments-mechani sms/instruments/international-covenant-civil-and-political-rights.

Iorio, Jorge, and Eliana Raszewski. 'Argentina Halts Export Registration for Soy Oil, Meal'. *Reuters,* 14 March 2022, sec. Americas. www.reuters. com/world/americas/argentina-halts-export-registration-soy-oil-meal-2022-03-14/.

Ishay, Micheline. *The History of Human Rights: From Ancient Times to the Globalization Era.* Berkeley: University of California Press, 2004.

Jacobsen, Peter. 'Opinion: Even the Courts Agree: Injunctions Should Not Prevent Journalists from Doing Their Jobs'. *The Globe and Mail,* 24 November 2021. www.theglobeandmail.com/opinion/arti cle-even-the-courts-agree-injunctions-should-not-prevent-journali sts-from/.

Johnston, Jane, and Anne Wallace. 'Who Is a Journalist? Changing Legal Definitions in a de-Territorialised Media Space'. *Digital Journalism* 5, no. 7 (2016): 850–67.
Jones, Tom. 'Should Journalists Be Allowed to Protest? A Legendary News Organization Tries to Address That Issue'. *Poynter (blog)*, 30 July 2021. www.poynter.org/commentary/2021/should-journalists-be-allowed-to-protest-a-legendary-news-organization-tries-to-address-that-issue/.
Josephi, Beate, Folker Hanusch, Martin Oller Alonso, Ivor Shapiro, Kenneth Andresen , Arnold S. De Beer, Abit Hoxha, et al. 'Profiles of Journalists: Demographic and Employment Patterns'. In *Worlds of Journalism: Comparing Journalistic Cultures across the Globe.*, edited by Thomas Hanitzsch, Folker Hanusch, Jyotika Ramaprasad, and Arnold S. De Beer. New York: Columbia University Press, 2019.
Josephi, Beate, and Penny O'Donnell. 'The Blurring Line between Freelance Journalists and Self-Employed Media Workers'. *Journalism*, 10 May 2022, 14648849221086806. https://doi.org/10.1177/1464884922 1086806.
Karlsson, Michael, Raul Ferrer Conill, and Henrik Örnebring. 'Recoding Journalism: Establishing Normative Dimensions for a Twenty-First Century News Media'. *Journalism Studies*, 5 January 2023, 1–20. https://doi.org/10.1080/1461670X.2022.2161929.
'Kashmir: India Top Court Orders Review of Longest Internet Shutdown'. *BBC News*, 10 January 2020, sec. India. www.bbc.com/news/world-asia-india-51058759.
'Kashmir Updates: Rajya Sabha Passes Bill That Divides J&K, Ladakh with 125 Votes in Favour, 61 against'. *Business Today'*, 5 August 2019. www.businesstoday.in/latest/economy-politics/story/kashmir-turmoil-live-updates-schools-colleges-closed-mobile-service-suspended-sect ion-144-imposed-in-jk-220031-2019-08-05.
Khumalo and Others v Holomisa, 2002 (5) SA 401 (CC) (South Africa: Constitutional Court 2002).
Klonick, Kate. 'Inside the Making of Facebook's Supreme Court'. *The New Yorker*, 12 February 2021. www.newyorker.com/tech/annals-of-tec hnology/inside-the-making-of-facebooks-supreme-court.
Kohler, Jeremy. 'St. Louis Can Banish People From Entire Neighborhoods. Police Can Arrest Them If They Come Back'. *ProPublica*, 1 December 2022. www.propublica.org/article/st-louis-can-banish-people-from-ent ire-neighborhoods.
Koji, T. 'Emerging Hierarchy in International Human Rights and Beyond: From the Perspective of Non-Derogable Rights'. *European Journal of International Law* 12, no. 5 (1 December 2001): 917–41. https://doi.org/10.1093/ejil/12.5.917.

References

Korpisaari, Päivi. 'The Journalistic Exemption in Personal Data Processing'. *Artificial Intelligence and the Media*, 15 February 2022, 61–91.

Kovach, Bill, and Tom Rosenstiel. *The Elements of Journalism: What Newspeople Should Know and the Public Should Expect*. 1st ed. New York: Three Rivers Press, 2001.

Krämer, Benjamin, and Klara Langmann. 'Professionalism as a Response to Right-Wing Populism? An Analysis of a Metajournalistic Discourse'. *International Journal of Communication* 14, no. 0 (30 October 2020): 23.

Kubens, Valerie. 'Setesdølens Redaktør Bøyer Ikke Av for Verken Boikott Eller Press—Fvn.No'. *Faerelandsvennen*. 11 November 2016. www.fvn.no/magasin/i/d9GgO/setesdoelens-redaktoer-boeyer-ikke-av-for-verken-boikott-eller-press.

Lamer, Wiebke. *Press Freedom as an International Human Right*. Cham: Springer, 2018.

Lawton v. Canada (Leaders' Debates Commission), 2019 FC 1424 (Federal Court of Canada 2019).

Lê Hoàng. 'Salon Tóc Di Động Dành Cho Người Nghèo'. *VNExpress*, 3 December 2022. https://vnexpress.net/salon-toc-di-dong-danh-cho-nguoi-ngheo-4543536.html.

Lederman, Marsha. 'Canadian Amber Bracken Wins World Press Photo of the Year for Residential School Memorial Photo'. *The Globe and Mail*, 7 April 2022. www.theglobeandmail.com/arts/art-and-architecture/article-canadian-photojournalist-amber-bracken-wins-world-press-photo-of-the/.

Lewis, Seth C. 'The Tension Between Professional Control and Open Participation'. *Information, Communication & Society* 15, no. 6 (1 August 2012): 836–66. https://doi.org/10.1080/1369118X.2012.674150.

Lichtenberg, Judith. 'Foundations and Limits of Freedom of the Press'. *Philosophy & Public Affairs* 16, no. 4 (1987): 329–55.

Lien, Ole Birger. 'Kyrkjetenar har fått sparken'. *Setesdølen*, 25 May 2021. www.setesdolen.no/nytt/kyrkjetenar-har-fatt-sparken/.

Lindgren, April, and Jon Corbett. 'Local News Map Data—January 2022'. *The Local News* Research Project, 5 January 2022. https://localnewsresearchproject.ca/2022/10/13/local-news-map-data-reports/.

Lindgren, April, Steph Wechsler, and Christina Wong. 'The COVID Years: Risk, Reward and Rethinking Priorities'. *J-Source*, 26 August 2022. https://j-source.ca/the-covid-years-risk-reward-and-rethinking-priorities/.

'List of Qualifying Digital News Subscriptions'. Canada.ca. Accessed 9 September 2022. www.canada.ca/en/revenue-agency/services/tax/individuals/topics/about-your-tax-return/tax-return/completing-a-tax-return/deductions-credits-expenses/deductions-credits-expenses/digital-news-subscription/list-qualifying-digital-news-subscriptions.html.

Lorca, Arnulf Becker. 'Human Rights in International Law? The Forgotten Origins of Human Rights in Latin America'. *The University of Toronto Law Journal* 67, no. 4 (2017): 465–95.

Ma, Siyuan, Daniel Bergan, Suhwoo Ahn, Dustin Carnahan, Nate Gimby, Johnny McGraw, and Isabel Virtue. 'Fact-Checking as a Deterrent? A Conceptual Replication of the Influence of Fact-Checking on the Sharing of Misinformation by Political Elites'. *Human Communication Research*, 15 December 2022, hqac031. https://doi.org/10.1093/hcr/hqac031.

Mackintosh. 'Indonesia Set to Punish Sex before Marriage with Jail Time'. *BBC News*, 2 December 2022. www.bbc.com/news/world-asia-63838213.

Macklem, Patrick. *The Sovereignty of Human Rights*. Oxford [UK]; New York, NY: Oxford University Press, 2015.

Malik, Asmaa, and Ivor Shapiro. 'What's Digital? What's Journalism?' In *The Routledge Companion to Digital Journalism Studies*, edited by Bob Franklin and Scott Eldridge II, 15–24. Routledge, 2017.

Malone, Clare. 'Dean Baquet Never Wanted to Be an Editor'. *The New Yorker*, 18 February 2022. www.newyorker.com/news/the-new-yorker-interview/dean-baquet-never-wanted-to-be-an-editor.

Mandela, Nelson. *Conversations with Myself*. Toronto: Doubleday Canada, 2011. www.overdrive.com/search?q=F866378C-8626-49FC-94BB-656DDA275EAF.

Maréchal, Nathalie, and Ellery Roberts Biddle. 'It's the Business Model: How Big Tech's Profit Machine Is Distorting the Public Sphere and Threatening Democracy'. *Ranking Digital Rights*, n.d.

Márquez-Ramírez, Mireya, Claudia Mellado, María Luisa Humanes, Adriana Amado, Daniel Beck, Sergey Davydov, Jacques Mick, et al. 'Detached or Interventionist? Comparing the Performance of Watchdog Journalism in Transitional, Advanced and Non-Democratic Countries'. *The International Journal of Press/Politics* 25, no. 1 (1 January 2020): 53–75. https://doi.org/10.1177/1940161219872155.

Martin, Robert W.T. 'From the "free and Open" Press to the "Press of Freedom": Liberalism, Republicanism and Early American Press Liberty'. *History of Political Thought* 15, no. 4 (1994): 505–34.

Masuku, John. 'Total Media Self-Regulation in Africa Still to Be Achieved'. *RedTech (blog)*, 14 October 2022. www.redtech.pro/total-media-self-regulation-in-africa-still-to-be-achieved/.

Mattar, Pacinthe. 'Objectivity Is a Privilege Afforded to White Journalists'. *The Walrus*, 21 August 2020. https://thewalrus.ca/objectivity-is-a-privilege-afforded-to-white-journalists/.

Mellado, Claudia, and Alfred Hermida. 'The Promoter, Celebrity, and Joker Roles in Journalists' Social Media Performance'. *Social Media*

+ *Society* 7, no. 1 (January 2021): 205630512199064. https://doi.org/10.1177/2056305121990643.

Mellado, Claudia, Cornelia Mothes, Daniel C. Hallin, María Luisa Humanes, Maria Lauber, Jacques Mick, Henry Silke, et al. 'Investigating the Gap between Newspaper Journalists' Role Conceptions and Role Performance in Nine European, Asian, and Latin American Countries'. *The International Journal of Press/Politics* 25, no. 4 (October 2020): 552–75. https://doi.org/10.1177/1940161220910106.

Meng, Jing, and Shixin Ivy Zhang. 'Contested Journalistic Professionalism in China: Journalists' Discourses in a Time of Crisis'. *Journalism Studies* 0, no. 0 (20 October 2022): 1–15. https://doi.org/10.1080/1461670X.2022.2135581.

Merrill, John C. 'Professionalization: Danger to Freedom and Pluralism'. *Journal of Mass Media Ethics* 1, no. 2 (1986): 56–60.

'Método de verificatión del debate público'. *Chequeado*. Accessed 7 October 2022. https://chequeado.com/metodo/.

Meurant, L.H. *Sixty Years Ago, or, Reminiscences of the Struggle for the Freedom of the Press in South Africa and the Establishment of the First Newspaper in the Eastern Province.* Cape Town: Saul Solomon, 1885. https://nlsa.on.worldcat.org/oclc/31710531.

Miami Herald Pub. Co. v. Tornillo, 418 U.S. 241 (1974).

Midori, Aoki. 'Japanese, Australian Students Bond Where Their Countries Once Fought'. *NHK World*, 19 October 2022. www3.nhk.or.jp/nhkworld/en/news/backstories/2117/.

Mieth, D. 'The Basic Norm of Truthfulness: Its Ethical Justification and Universality'. In *Communication Ethics and Universal Values*, edited by C. Christians and M. Traber, 87–104. SAGE Publications Ltd, 1997. https://dx.doi.org/10.4135/9781452243542.

Mill, John Stuart. *On Liberty*. Project Gutenberg, 2001. London: Walter Scott, 1901. www.gutenberg.org/files/34901/34901-h/34901-h.htm.

Milosavljević, Marko, Melita Poler, and Rok Čeferin. 'In the Name of the Right to Be Forgotten: New Legal and Policy Issues and Practices Regarding Unpublishing Requests in Slovenian Online News Media'. *Digital Journalism* 0, no. 0 (15 April 2020): 1–17. https://doi.org/10.1080/21670811.2020.1747942.

Miyagawa, Shigeru, Cora Lesure, and Vitor A. Nóbrega. 'Cross-Modality Information Transfer: A Hypothesis about the Relationship among Prehistoric Cave Paintings, Symbolic Thinking, and the Emergence of Language'. *Frontiers in Psychology* 9 (20 February 2018): 115. https://doi.org/10.3389/fpsyg.2018.00115.

Moore, Suzanne. 'On Social Media Everyone Is a Hero or Zero. We Must Embrace the Complexity of Real Life'. *The Guardian*, 19 October 2020, sec. Opinion. www.theguardian.com/commentisfree/2020/oct/19/on-social-media-everyone-is-a-hero-or-zero-we-must-embrace-the-complexity-of-real-life.

Moreno-Gil, Victoria, Xavier Ramon, and Ruth Rodríguez-Martínez. 'Fact-Checking Interventions as Counteroffensives to Disinformation Growth: Standards, Values, and Practices in Latin America and Spain'. *Media and Communication* 9, no. 1 (3 March 2021): 251–63. https://doi.org/10.17645/mac.v9i1.3443.

Mounck, Yascha. 'How To Avoid High Conflict'. *Persuasion (blog)*, 22 May 2021. www.persuasion.community/p/-how-to-avoid-high-conflict#details.

Mounk, Yascha. 'You Just Won't Understand!' *Persuasion* (blog), 11 September 2021. www.persuasion.community/p/-you-just-wont-understand.

'Mountain Ink; Home'. Accessed 17 November 2022. https://mountain-ink.com/.

Müller, Karsten, and Carlo Schwarz. 'Fanning the Flames of Hate: Social Media and Hate Crime'. *Journal of the European Economic Association* 19, no. 4 (11 August 2021): 2131–67. https://doi.org/10.1093/jeea/jvaa045.

Mullin, Benjamin. 'Read Carl Bernstein and Bob Woodward's Remarks to the White House Correspondents' Association'. *Poynter (blog)*, 30 April 2017. www.poynter.org/reporting-editing/2017/read-carl-bernstein-and-bob-woodwards-remarks-to-the-white-house-correspondents-association/.

Nafría, Ismael. 'How Argentine Innovators Created Chequeado and Made It a Global Leader in Fact-Checking'. *Knight Centre: LatAm Journalism Review*, 8 January 2018. https://latamjournalismreview.org/articles/how-argentine-innovators-created-chequeado-and-made-it-a-global-leader-in-fact-checking/.

Napoli, Philip M. *Audience Evolution: New Technologies and the Transformation of Media Audiences.* New York, N.Y: Columbia University Press, 2011.

Neth, Sybille. 'Spendenaktion Hilfe Für Den Nachbarn: Streit Um Die Rente Zehrt an Den Nerven—Hilfe Für Den Nachbarn'. *Stuttgarter Zeitung*, 2 December 2022. www.stuttgarter-zeitung.de/inhalt.spendenaktion-hilfe-fuer-den-nachbarn-streit-um-die-rente-zehrt-an-den-nerven.7a556af3-3cbe-4cb0-ac62-8598f49bec3a.html.

Newman, Nic. 'Journalism, Media, and Technology Trends and Predictions 2022'. *Reuters Institute for the Study of Journalism*, 10 January 2022. https://reutersinstitute.politics.ox.ac.uk/journalism-media-and-technology-trends-and-predictions-2022.

Newman, Nic, Richard Fletcher, Craig T. Robertson, Kirsten Eddy, and Rasmus Kleis Nielsen. 'Digital News Report 2022'. Reuters Institute for the Study of Journalism. Accessed 27 October 2022. https://reutersinstitute.politics.ox.ac.uk/digital-news-report/2022/interactive.

Newman, Nic, Richard Fletcher, Anne Schulz, Simge Andı, Craig T. Robertson, and Rasmus Kleis Nielsen. 'Digital News Report 2021'. Reuters Institute for the Study of Journalism, 2021. https://reutersinstitute.politics.ox.ac.uk/digital-news-report/2021.

Newton, Lisa H., Louis Hodges, and Susan Keith. 'Accountability in the Professions: Accountability in Journalism'. *Journal of Mass Media Ethics* 19, no. 3 (2004): 166–90.

Nimmer, Melville B. 'Introduction--Is Freedom of the Press a Redundancy: What Does It Add to Freedom of Speech?' *Hastings Law Journal* 26, no. 3 (1975): 639–58.

Nix, Naomi. 'Facebook, Twitter Dismantle a U.S. Influence Campaign about Ukraine'. *Washington Post,* 24 August 2022. www.washingtonpost.com/technology/2022/08/24/facebook-twitter-us-influence-campaign-ukraine/.

Oliver, Laura. 'The Fight for Facts in the Global South: How Four Projects Are Building a New Model'. *Reuters Institute for the Study of Journalism,* 30 September 2021. https://reutersinstitute.politics.ox.ac.uk/news/fight-facts-global-south-how-four-projects-are-building-new-model.

Oller Alonso, Martin, Ivor Shapiro, et al. 'Defining the Worlds of Journalism Study Sample'. Worlds of Journalism Study, November 2019. https://worldsofjournalism.org/wp-content/uploads/2020/03/WJS3_Definitions_working_paper.pdf.

Oremus, Will. 'What Substack Is Really Doing to the Media'. *Slate,* 23 April 2021. https://slate.com/business/2021/04/substack-media-new-york-times-subscriptions-poaching.html.

Pan American Union. *Report on the Results of the Conference: Eighth International Conference of American States, Lima, Peru, December 9–27, 1938.* Literary Licensing, LLC, 2013.

Patterson, Thomas E., and Wolfgang Donsbach. 'News Decisions: Journalists as Partisan Actors'. *Political Communication* 13, no. 4 (1 October 1996): 455–68. https://doi.org/10.1080/10584609.1996.9963131.

Perelló, Carlos Felipe Amunátegui. 'On Supernatural Law: About the Origins of Human Rights and Natural Law in Antiquity'. *Fundamina* 20, no. 1 (January 2014): 15–26.

Perreault, Gregory. *Digital Journalism and the Facilitation of Hate.* Routledge, 2022.

Perreault, Gregory, and Kaitlin Miller. 'When Journalists Are Voiceless: How Lifestyle Journalists Cover Hate and Mitigate Harassment'.

Journalism Studies 23, no. 15 (18 November 2022): 1977–93. https://doi.org/10.1080/1461670X.2022.2135583.

Petkova, Bilyana. 'Towards an Internal Hierarchy of Values in the EU Legal Order: Balancing the Freedom of Speech and Data Privacy—Bilyana Petkova, 2016'. *Maastricht Journal of European and Comparative Law* 23 (1 June 2016). https://doi.org/10.1177/1023263X1602300303.

Pinsker, Joe. 'We're Learning the Wrong Lessons From the World's Happiest Countries'. *The Atlantic*, 27 June 2021. www.theatlantic.com/family/archive/2021/06/worlds-happiest-countries-denmark-finland-norway/619299/.

Pityana, N. Barney et al. 'Faultlines: Inquiry into Racism in the Media'. South African Human Rights Commission, August 2000. www.sahrc.org.za/home/21/files/Reports/Racismin%20the%20media.pdf2000.pdf.

Plessing, Julia. 'Shifting the South African Media Diversity Debate from the Stick to the Carrot: Lessons from Scandinavia, Latin America and West Africa | Scholars Portal Journals'. *African Journalism Studies* 38, no. 1 (January 2017): 66–84. https://doi.org/10.1080/23743670.2017.1288645.

Ponsford, Dominic. 'Julian Assange Verdict: Extradition Denied over Suicide Fear'. Press Gazette, 4 January 2021. www.pressgazette.co.uk/julian-assange-extradition-trial-verdict-decision-expected-today/.

Porter, Ethan, and Thomas J. Wood. 'The Global Effectiveness of Fact-Checking: Evidence from Simultaneous Experiments in Argentina, Nigeria, South Africa, and the United Kingdom'. *Proceedings of the National Academy of Sciences* 118, no. 37 (14 September 2021): e2104235118. https://doi.org/10.1073/pnas.2104235118.

Preston, Paschal. *Making the News: Journalism and News Cultures in Europe*. London: Routledge, 2008.

Protection of Personal Information Act, South Africa § (2013).

Puijk, Roel, Eli Beate Hestnes, Simon Holm, Andrea Jakobsen, and Marianne Myrdal. 'Local Newspapers' Transition to Online Publishing and Video Use: Experiences from Norway'. *Journalism Studies* 22, no. 9 (4 July 2021): 1123–41. https://doi.org/10.1080/1461670X.2021.1922303.

Quinlan, The Hon. Peter. 'The Rule of Law in a Social Media Age [Sir Francis Burt Oration]', 2022. www.supremecourt.wa.gov.au/_files/Speeches/2022/TheRuleofLawinaSocialMediaAgeSirFrancisBurtOration2022.pdf.

Ramaprasad, Jyotika, Thomas Hanitzsch, Epp Lauk, Halliki Harro-Loit, Jan Fredrik Hovden, Jari Väliverronen, and Stephanie Craft. 'Ethical Considerations: Journalists' Perceptions of Professional Practice'. In *Worlds of Journalism: Comparing Journalistic Cultures across the Globe.*, edited by Thomas Hanitzsch, Folker Hanusch, Jyotika Ramaprasad, and Arnold S. De Beer. New York: Columbia University Press, 2019.

Rauhala, Emily. 'Norway Is Portrayed as Both Hero and Villain in Europe's Energy Crisis'. *Washington Post,* 8 October 2022, sec. Europe. www.washingtonpost.com/world/2022/10/08/norway-gas-prices-supply-europe/.

Re Brake; Anderson v. Nalcor Energy, 2019 NLCA 17 (Court of Appeal of Newfoundland and Labrador 2019).

Rebel News Network Ltd. v. Canada (Leaders' Debates Commission), 2022 FC 313 (Federal Court of Canada 2022).

'Rebel News Is Suing Justin Trudeau'. Accessed 28 May 2022. www.rebelnews.com/rebel_news_is_suing_justin_trudeau.

Rech, Marcelo. 'Brazil's Riots Highlight the Need for a Global Antidote to Disinformation'. *The Globe and Mail,* 21 January 2023. www.theglobeandmail.com/opinion/article-brazils-riots-highlight-the-need-for-a-global-antidote-to/.

Reporters Without Borders (RSF). 'RSF Press Freedom Index, 2022'. Accessed 17 October 2022. https://rsf.org/en/index.

Reporters Without Borders (RSF). 'RSF's 2022 World Press Freedom Index: A New Era of Polarisation'. Accessed 17 October 2022. https://rsf.org/en/rsf-s-2022-world-press-freedom-index-new-era-polarisation-0.

Reus-Smit, Christian. 'Human Rights in a Global Ecumene'. *International Affairs* 87, no. 5 (28 September 2011): 1205–18.

Reynolds v. *Times Newspapers Limited and Others (United Kingdom House of Lords* 1999).

Riera, Ariel, and Laura Zommer. 'Using Fact Checking to Improve Information Systems in Argentina'. *The Political Quarterly* 91, no. 3 (2020): 600–604. https://doi.org/10.1111/1467-923X.12895.

'Rights and duties of the editor'. Association of Norwegian Editors and Norwegian Media Businesses' *Association.* Accessed 7 November 2022. www.nored.no/Redaktoeransvar/Redaktoerplakaten/Redaktoerplakaten-engelsk.

Rokeach, Milton. *The Nature of Human Values.* Free Press, 1973.

Roy, Arundhati. 'The Hanging of Afzal Guru Is a Stain on India's Democracy'. *The Guardian*, 10 February 2013. www.theguardian.com/commentisfree/2013/feb/10/hanging-afzal-guru-india-democracy.

Sacasas, L.M. 'The Analog City and the Digital City'. *The New Atlantis*, Winter 2020. www.thenewatlantis.com/publications/the-analog-city-and-the-digital-city.

Sackur, Stephen. 'Maria Ressa and Dmitry Muratov: Fighting for a Free Press'. *BBC HARDtalk.* Accessed 15 December 2021. www.bbc.co.uk/sounds/play/w3ct1nc9.

Satchwell, Kathleen, Nikiwe Bikitsha, and Rich Mkhondo. 'Independent Panel Report: Inquiry into Media Athics and Credibility'. South African National Editors' Forum (SANEF), April 2021. https://sanef.org.za/programmes/media-ethics-and-credibility-inquiry/.

Saunders, Doug. 'Opinion: The Christchurch Massacre May Have Had a Canadian Connection—but There's a Reason You May Not Know about It'. *The Globe and Mail*, 15 March 2022. www.theglobeandmail.com/opinion/article-the-christchurch-massacre-may-have-had-a-canadian-connection-but/.

Schiffrin, Anya. 'Credibility and Trust in Journalism'. In *The Oxford Encyclopedia of Journalism Studies*, edited by Henrik Örnebring. Oxford New York: Oxford university press, 2020.

Schmidt, Christine. 'Unprepared for Unpublishing? Here's How Some Newsrooms Are Rethinking What Lasts Forever'. *Nieman Lab (blog)*, 4 September 2019. www.niemanlab.org/2019/09/unprepared-for-unpublishing-heres-how-some-newsrooms-are-rethinking-what-lasts-forever/.

Schneider, Gabe. 'What Does Movement Journalism Mean for Journalism as a Whole?' *The Objective (blog)*, 16 April 2021. https://objectivejournalism.org/2021/04/what-does-movement-journalism-mean-for-journalism-as-a-whole/.

Schroeder, Jared. *The Press Clause and Digital Technology's Fourth Wave: Media Law and the Symbiotic Web*. Routledge, 2020.

Schudson, Michael. 'The Objectivity Norm in American Journalism'. *Journalism* 2, no. 2 (1 August 2001): 149–70.

———. *The Sociology of News. Contemporary Societies*. New York: Norton, 2002.

———. *Why Democracies Need an Unlovable Press*. Malden, MA: Polity, 2008.

Schultz, Ida. 'The Journalistic Gut Feeling'. *Journalism Practice* 1, no. 2 (2007): 190–207. https://doi.org/10.1080/17512780701275507.

Scrire, Sarah. 'The New York Times' New Opinion Editor, Kathleen Kingsbury, on Reimagining Opinion Journalism'. *Nieman Lab (blog)*, 11 February 2021. www.niemanlab.org/2021/02/the-new-york-times-opinion-editor-kathleen-kingsbury-on-reimagining-opinion-journalism/.

Setesdølen. 'Setesdølen braut god presseskikk', 3 February 2022. www.setesdolen.no/nytt/setesdolen-braut-god-presseskikk/.

Shapiro, Ivor. 'Evaluating Journalism: Towards an Assessment Framework for the Practice of Journalism'. *Journalism Practice* 4, no. 2 (2010): 143–62. https://doi.org/10.1080/17512780903306571.

———. 'Toward an International Perspective on Media Accountability'. In *La Regulation Du Travail Journalistique Dans Dix Pays, Dont Le Canada*, edited by Daniel Giroux and Pierre Trudel. Sainte-Foy, Québec: Centre d'études sur les medias, 2014.

Shapiro, Ivor, Colette Brin, Isabelle Bédard-Brûlé, and Kasia Mychajlowycz. 'Verification as a Strategic Ritual'. *Journalism Practice* 7, no. 6 (2013): 657–73. https://doi.org/10.1080/17512786.2013.765638.

Shapiro, Ivor, Colette Brin, Phiiippa Spoel, and Lee Marshall. 'Images of Essence: Journalists' Discourse on the Professional "Discipline of Verification"'. *Canadian Journal of CommunicatIon* 41, no. 1 (2016). https://cjc.utpjournals.press/doi/full/10.22230/cjc.2016v41n1a2929

Shapiro, Ivor, and Brian MacLeod Rogers. 'Who Owns the News? The "Right to Be Forgotten" and Journalists' Conflicting Principles'. In *Who Owns the News? The 'Right to Be Forgotten' and Journalists' Conflicting Principles*, edited by Scott Eldridge II and Bob Franklin. Routledge Handbooks Online, 2018. https://doi.org/10.4324/9781315270449-25.

Shapiro, Ivor, Lisa Taylor, and Edward Tubb. 'Press Councils in Canada: Models of Practice and Prospects for Alternatives. [Report on a Study for Newspapers Canada]'. Toronto: Ryerson Journalism Research Centre, 16 October 2012. https://doi.org/10.32920/ryerson.21432999.v1.

Shin, Jieun, and Kjerstin Thorson. 'Partisan Selective Sharing: The Biased Diffusion of Fact-Checking Messages on Social Media'. *Journal of Communication* 67, no. 2 (2017): 233–55. https://doi.org/10.1111/jcom.12284.

Shoemaker, Pamela J., and Stephen D. Reese. *Mediating the Message in the 21st Century: A Media Sociology Perspective*. Third edition. New York: Routledge, 2014.

Siebert, Fred, Theodore Bernard Peterson, Theodore Peterson, and Wilbur Schramm. *Four Theories of the Press: The Authoritarian, Libertarian, Social Responsibility, and Soviet Communist Concepts of What the Press Should Be and Do*. University of Illinois Press, 1956.

Simonton, Anna. 'Out of Struggle: Strengthening and Expanding Movement Journalism in the U.S. South'. *Project South*, 2017. https://projectsouth.org/movement-journalism/.

Singer, Jane. 'Journalism and Digital Technologies'. In *Changing the News: The Forces Shaping Journalism in Uncertain Times*, edited by Wilson Lowrey and Peter J. Gade. New York: Routledge, 2011.

Skuncke, Marie-Christine. 'Freedom of the Press and Social Equality in Sweden, 1766–1772'. In *Scandinavia in the Age of Revolution: Nordic Political Cultures, 1740–1820*, edited by Michael Bregnsbo, Pasi Ihalainen, and Patrik Winton. London: Routledge, 2016.

Slaatta, Tore. 'Print versus Digital in Norwegian Newspapers'. *Media, Culture & Society* 37, no. 1 (1 January 2015): 124–33. https://doi.org/10.1177/0163443714553566.

Smith, Ben. 'Heather Cox Richardson Offers a Break From the Media Maelstrom. It's Working'. *The New York Times*, 28 December 2020, sec. Business. www.nytimes.com/2020/12/27/business/media/heather-cox-richardson-substack-boston-college.html.

———. 'Why We're Freaking Out About Substack'. *The New York Times*, 11 April 2021, sec. Business. www.nytimes.com/2021/04/11/business/media/substack-newsletter-competition.html.

Solomon, Salem. 'When Wire Services Make Mistakes, Misinformation Spreads Quickly'. *Poynter (blog)*, 12 March 2018. www.poynter.org/fact-checking/2018/when-wire-services-make-mistakes-misinformation-spreads-quickly/.

'Status of Ratification: Interactive Dashboard'. *United Nations*. 13 January 2022. https://indicators.ohchr.org/.

Stearns, Josh. 'Acts of Journalism: Defining Press Freedom in the Digital Age'. *Freepress*, October 2013. www.freepress.net/news/updates/new-call-protect-acts-journalism.

Stephen, Leslie. 'Chatham, Francis, and Junius'. *The English Historical Review* 3, no. 10 (1888): 233–49.

Taibbi, Matt, and Daniel Medina. 'The New York Times Editorial Board's Creepy Avengers Fantasy'. Substack newsletter. *TK News by Matt Taibbi* (blog), 22 November 2022. https://taibbi.substack.com/p/the-new-york-times-editorial-boards.

'[The Freedom Charter, 1955 [Documents on Democracy: South Africa]'. *Journal of Democracy* 1, no. 4 (Fall 1990): 128–34.

'The Independence Party Hosts Leadership Debate Featuring Artur Pawlowski'. Accessed 9 September 2022. *Rebel News*. www.rebelnews.com/the_independence_party_hosts_leadership_debate_featuring_artur_pawlowski.

'The Status of Journalists in Europe: Resolution 2213 of the Parliamentary Assembly of the Council of Europe', 26 February 2018. https://pace.coe.int/en/files/24735#trace-5.

Toff, Benjamin, Sumitra Badrinathan, Camila Mont'Alverne, Amy Ross Arguedas, Richard Fletcher, and Rasmus Kleis Nielsen. 'Listening to What Trust in News Means to Users: Qualitative Evidence from Four Countries', April 2021, 52.

Tuchman, Gaye. 'Objectivity as Strategic Ritual: An Examination of Newsmen's Notions of Objectivity'. *The American Journal of Sociology* 77, no. 4 (January 1972): 660–79.

Uleberg, Odd-Inge Rønning. 'Haugsgjerd Har Vore Bladstyrar i 39 År'. *Faerelandsvennen*. 19 January 2015. www.fvn.no/nyheter/lokalt/i/6gz1W/haugsgjerd-har-vore-bladstyrar-i-39-aar.

'Universal Declaration of Human Rights'. United Nations. Accessed 19 February 2022. www.un.org/en/about-us/universal-declaration-of-human-rights.

van Dalen, Arjen, Erik Albæk, and Claes de Vreese. 'Suspicious Minds: Explaining Political Cynicism among Political Journalists in Europe'. *European Journal of Communication* 26, no. 2 (1 June 2011): 147–62. https://doi.org/10.1177/0267323111404841.

Vice, John, and Stephen Farrell. 'The History of Hansard'. House of Lords. Accessed 5 February 2020. www.parliament.uk/globalassets/documents/lords-library/History-of-Hansard.pdf.

Vienna Declaration and Programme of Action. Accessed 21 October 2022. www.ohchr.org/en/instruments-mechanisms/instruments/vienna-declaration-and-programme-action.

Waisbord, Silvio. 'Truth Is What Happens to News: On Journalism, Fake News, and Post-Truth'. *Journalism Studies* 19, no. 13 (3 October 2018): 1866–78. https://doi.org/10.1080/1461670X.2018.1492881.

Wardle, Claire, and Hossein Derakhshan. 'Information Disorder: Toward an Interdisciplinary Framework for Research and Policy Making'. *Council of Europe*. 27 December 2017. https://rm.coe.int/informat ion-disorder-toward-an-interdisciplinary-framework-for-researc/168 076277c.

Wasserman, Herman. 'The State of South African Media: A Space to Contest Democracy'. *Publizistik* 65, no. 3 (1 August 2020): 451–65. https://doi.org/10.1007/s11616-020-00594-4.

Watson, H.G. 'National Newsmedia Council Aims to Bring More Media into the Fold'. *J-Source,* 25 November 2015. https://j-source.ca/national-newsmedia-council-aims-to-bring-more-media-into-the-fold/.

'Wet'suwet'en Camp Leader, Journalists Arrested as RCMP Enforce Pipeline Injunction in Northern B.C.'. *CBC News*, 20 November 2021. www.cbc.ca/news/canada/british-columbia/15-arrests-journalists-wet suweten-cgl-1.6256696.

White, David Manning. 'The Gatekeeper: A Case Study in the Selection of News'. *Journalism Quarterly* 27, no. 4 (1950): 383–90. https://doi.org/10.1177/107769905002700403.

WIC Radio Ltd. v. Simpson, No. 2008 SCC 40 (Supreme Court of Canada).

Williams, Matthew L, Pete Burnap, Amir Javed, Han Liu, and Sefa Ozalp. 'Hate in the Machine: Anti-Black and Anti-Muslim Social Media Posts as Predictors of Offline Racially and Religiously Aggravated Crime'. *The British Journal of Criminology,* 23 July 2019, azz049. https://doi.org/10.1093/bjc/azz049.

Wilson-Lee, Edward. 'Killing the Messenger: Diplomatic Translators in Late Elizabethan Culture'. *Huntington Library Quarterly* 82, no. 4 (2019): 579–95. https://doi.org/10.1353/hlq.2019.0024.

Winston, Brian, and Matthew Winston. *The Roots of Fake News Objecting to Objective Journalism*, 2021.
'World: Abuses in Real Time'. *Reporters Without Borders (RSF)*. Accessed 25 November 2022. https://rsf.org/en/barometer.
Wright, Jack. 'Nobel Peace Prize Winner Malala Yousafzai Is Trolled on Social Media'. *Mail Online,* 16 October 2020, sec. News. www.dailymail.co.uk/news/article-8847173/Nobel-Peace-Prize-winner-Malala-Yousafzai-trolled-social-media.html.
Wright, Shelley. *International Human Rights, Decolonisation and Globalisation: Becoming Human*. Routledge Studies in International Law 3. London; New York: Routledge, 2001.
Yangming He. 'Hangzhou, the Origins of the World Press and Journalism?' *Journalism Studies* 16, no. 4 (4 July 2015): 547–61. https://doi.org/10.1080/1461670X.2014.930239.
Zaffarano, Francesco. '[Interview] Marcela Duarte: Head of Product—Agência Lupa'. *Mapping Journalism (blog)*, 3 January 2023. https://mappingjournalism.substack.com/p/how-lupa-is-fighting-disinformation.
Zahay, Megan L., Kelly Jensen, Yiping Xia, and Sue Robinson. 'The Labor of Building Trust: Traditional and Engagement Discourses for Practicing Journalism in a Digital Age'. *Journalism & Mass Communication Quarterly* 98, no. 4 (2021): 1041–58.

Index

Note: Endnotes are indicated by the page number followed by "n" and the note number e.g., 52n66 refers to note 66 on page 52.

access to restricted spaces 36–7, 39, 51–2
accountability 88, 90–1, 95–6
accreditation and credentials 39–42, 44, 52
accuracy 71–3, 100; *see also* truth; facts
African National Congress (ANC) 26
African values 8
Akhoon, Adil Amin 97–8, 102–4
Al Jazeera 103
Alonso, Martin Oller xv, 52n66
amaBhungane 27–8
analytics 61, 110
apartheid xi–xii, 9–10, 16–18, 23–4
Argentina 54–6, 67–70
The Argus 25
artificial intelligence, robots 62, 100
Asante people 4
Asian values 8
Assange, Julian 51
assumptions 2, 15, 58, 73, 95, 112
audience behaviour and data *see* analytics
audience(s) 60–2, 71, 78; trust in news media 28, 45, 76, 90, 92–6, 100, 109, 110
Australia 27, 51, 91, 113

autonomy of journalists 15, 47, 66, 75, 81–2, 92, 106

Bastiat, Frédéric 36
Bell, Emily 61
Bentham, Jeremy 5
Berger, Guy xv, 107
Berlin, Isaiah 36n9
bias *see* impartiality
Bijleveld, Hildebrand P. 107
Blackstone, William 29–30
Blanchett, Nicole xv, 61, 110
boundary work 82–3
Bourdieu, Pierre 84
Bracken, Amber 34
Brazil 71, 99, 111–12
Brin, Colette xv
Britain *see* United Kingdom
Brooke, Heather 74–5
Brümmer, Stefaans xv, 25–7
business challenges and objectives *see* financial challenges

Cameron, Jamie xv, 13n34, 52n68
Canada xii, 33–6, 39–44, 52, 91, 113
"cancel culture" 3
censorship 21, 23, 29–32, 36, 47–8, 66, 99, 104; *see also* content moderation

Chase, Anthony 4
Chequeado 54–6, 67–71
China 84n25, 103
Chomsky, Noam 46
Christensen, Clayton 28–9
clickbait 69; *see also* analytics
climate change 2, 12, 40, 111
Code of Hammurabi 4
Cohen, Nicole 82, 109
common law 87
confidential sources 32, 36, 50–2, 101
consensus *see* facts
constitutions and constitutional law 4–9, 13, 25, 30–6, 38, 52, 81, 98; *see also* human rights
content moderation in social media 2, 33, 100
contingent rights and freedoms 37–8, 49
core rights or freedoms *see* fundamental rights
corrections *see* errors and corrections
Council of Europe 47, 50
Courts of law: access to and coverage of 15, 39, 107
Covid-19 41, 47, 89, 112
credentials *see* accreditation
credibility 28, 58, 61; *see also* trust
cultures 15, 57, 59–60, 85

Daily Maverick 27
data privacy 39, 86, 108
Declaration of the Rights of Man 5
defamation *see* libel
democracy xi, 25–7, 29, 30–1, 42–3, 46, 48–9, 62, 67, 83
Derakhshan, Hossein 47
de Peuter, Greig 82, 109
de Souza Godoi, Guilherme Canela xv
Die Burger 18, 27
Die Welt 31
disinformation *see* information disorder

disruption 28–9, 35, 43, 46, 55, 64, 75, 82, 93, 107
Dragomir, Marius 75–6
duties and obligations 7, 30, 36, 38, 49, 66, 71–4, 87–8, 100

Echaquan, Joyce xi
"echo chambers" and "filter bubbles" 45–6
enabling environment for newsgathering 30–2, 100, 102; *see also* financial challenges and suppor; local news
Egeberg, Kristoffer xv
Eliot, T.S. 7
entitlement *see* legal privileges
epistemology 5, 53, 63, 66; standpoint epistemology 64–6, 71, 74
errors and corrections 59–60, 65, 88, 94, 100, 101, 109; *see also* transparency
exemptions *see* legal privileges
European Commission 95
European Convention on Human Rights 11
European Court of Human Rights 107

Facebook 27, 44, 56; *see also* Meta
fact checking 55–6, 67, 70, 72; second-generation fact checking 71–2
facts and opinions 3, 30, 59, 66, 88, 106
facts, factual information 3, 17, 38, 42, 49, 57, 59–60, 62, 74, 87, 106–7; *see also* truth; verification
Fairbank, Viviane 73–4
Fædrelandsvennen 78
fake news *see* information disorder
filter bubbles *see* echo chambers
financial challenges and support for journalism and news organizations 2, 43–4, 104, 111; *see also* local news

Finland 28
First Amendment *see* United States
Floberghagen, Elin 96
4chan 48
Frantzen, Hege Iren xv
freedom of expression xii–xiii, 1–3, 6, 9–11, 25, 36, 38, 48, 51, 108; conditions and limits 11–15, 30, 32–6, 48; history and justifications 6–8, 10–11
freedom of the press: defining 15, 18–19, 30–2, 49, 51–2; conditions and limits 36–8, 104–6; history 19–23, 29–30; threats to 99–102
freelance journalists 46, 85, 98, 109; *see also* Akhoon; financial support; local journalism
fundamental rights and freedoms 7, 13–14, 31, 38

Gandhi, Mohandas K. (Mahatma) 6–7, 10
gatekeeping *see* news selection
gender 12, 25, 40, 63
Germany 95, 113
Gershberg, Zac 31
Ghana 4
Gillers, Stephen 42
Gilligan, Carol 8
Giménez, José 68–9
good faith 33–5, 107
Google 104, 111; *see also* YouTube (subsidiary)
governments: monitoring by journalists 29, 42, 55, 57, 59
Greig, George 22–3
Gutenberg, Johann 20
Guru, Azfal 102

Habermas, Jürgen 50
habits and rituals of journalists 60, 63, 66, 73, 95, 109–10
Hanitzsch, Thomas xiv, 57–9
Hansard, John 37
Hanusch, Folker xiv, 57–8
Harber, Anton xv, 24n21

harm 3, 14, 25, 42, 69; harm principle 9–13, 48; online harm 2, 47
hate and hate speech 2–3, 45–6, 48
Haugsgjerd, Sigurd 77–81, 89–90
Hodges, Louis 108
human rights 4–9, 13–14, 37, 67; *see also* fundamental rights; negative and positive rights
Huxley, Julian 6

Illing, Sean 31
impartiality, neutrality, objectivity 35, 50, 60–5, 71–5, 85, 94–5
India 20, 98–9, 102–4; *see also* Kashmir
Indonesia 112
information disorder, disinformation, fake news 2, 20, 40, 44–7, 61, 65, 69–71, 99, 105
instrumental rights 31–2, 38
investigative journalism 25–8
Inter-American Commission on Human Rights 13
International Covenant on Civil and Political Rights 30
Italy 99

Jensen, Arne xv
journalism and journalists; advocacy and opinion 40–1; definitions of 42, 49–52; history of 22–5; *see also* news, reporting
Junius 21, 23, 32, 104

Kashmir 97–8, 102–4
Kovach, Bill 60

labour contracts and rights *see* unions of journalists
La Nación 67
Langenhoven, Cornelis Jacobus 17
legal privileges for journalists xiv, 15–16, 25, 29–32, 35, 37–9, 52, 66, 107–8; *see also* access to restrictive spaces; confidential sources; defamation; enabling

environment; financial challenges
libel, defamation 12, 15, 21–2, 27, 32, 39, 74, 87; responsible-journalism defence 86–8
Lima agreement 6
Lincoln, Abraham 31
The Line 44
local news, news poverty, news deserts 43, 77–80, 84, 100–2, 105

Macklem, Patrick 8
Macri, Mauricio 67
The Mail and Guardian 25–8
mal-information *see* information disorder
Mandela, Nelson 17, 25
Meijer, Irene Costera 107
Mellado, Claudia 59
Meta 104, 111; *see also* Facebook; WhatsApp (subsidiaries)
Mill, John Stuart 10–11, 47
misinformation *see* information disorder
moderation *see* content moderation
Morocco 8
Mountain Ink 103
movement journalism 63
Muratov, Dmitry 106

national security 11, 30
natural rights 5, 31
negative and positive rights 36, 38–9, 66
Netherlands 27
neutrality *see* impartiality
New Lines Magazine 103
news 19; history of 19–21; newsgathering 30, 35, 37; *see also* local news; reporting
news poverty and news deserts *see* financial challenges; local news
news selection and newsworthiness 46, 49, 61–2, 95–6
News24 27
New Zealand 51
Nigeria 99, 112

Nkosi Silelel' i-Afrika 16
Nobel Peace Prize 44–5, 106
Norway 77–80, 88–92, 96; ethics codes and press council 90–1; journalists' and press associations 91, 96; press law 92

objectivity *see* impartiality
obligations *see* duties and obligations
Open Society 27
opinions 3, 9, 12, 30, 42, 45, 65–6, 87–8, 99, 106; *see also* facts and opinions; journalism
ownership *see* financial challenges; local news; publishers

Pan American Union 6
parliamentary press galleries 37, 39–41, 51
participative gatekeeping 61–2, 110n32; *see also* analytics
Paul, Louise vii, xv
peripheral journalists 52
Philippines 113
pluralism in news 46–7, 66
polarization xi, 2–3, 106, 45–6, 70, 92, 106
police xii, 24–5, 34–5, 38, 73, 99, 102–3
positive rights *see* negative and positive rights
precarity 82, 105, 109, 112; *see also* freelance journalists, local journalism; unions
the press *see* freedom of the press
press councils 41, 90–1, 89–91, 94, 101–2, 108
Prestvold, Janne B. xv, 78n1
professionalism, professionalization, professional standards 75, 81–8, 94, 99, 105, 107, 109
public broadcasters 79, 85, 93, 105; *see also* financial challenges and support
publishers 21, 23, 29, 46, 56, 63, 76, 81, 90–1, 95, 104–7, 109, 111

QAnon 48
Qoboza, Percy 24

race and antiracism 2–3, 6, 25–6, 46, 63
Rapport 18
Rawls, John 88
Rebel News 39–44
Rech, Marcelo 111
religions and beliefs 4, 6–8, 13–14, 20, 25, 32, 36
Reporters Without Borders (RSF) 27, 30, 95, 98–9
reporting *see* facts; news
reserved (versus universally applicable) rights 36–9, 66
"responsible journalism" *see* defamation
resources *see* financial challenges
Reuters Institute for the Study of Journalism 27, 80, 92–5
rhetoric 5, 65, 74, 83, 95
rights *see* human rights
Ripley, Amanda 45
rituals *see* habits and rituals of journalists
Rogers, Brian MacLeod vii, xv, 86n40
role performance 58–9, 95
Rollwagen, Heather xv
Rosenstiel, Tom 60
rule of law 12, 49
Russia 106

Sacasas, L. M. 47
safety and threats 12, 27, 30–1, 48, 51, 72, 75–6, 92, 97, 99, 102, 104
Saudi Arabia 7
self-regulation 76, 82, 91, 96, 108, 111
Setesdølen 78–80, 89–90
Shadows of Nazareth 17
Sharia law 8
shield laws *see* confidential sources
Skok, David 29
social media 2, 27–8, 46, 60–1, 68, 70; *see also* content moderation; echo chambers

Sohr, Olivia 55–6, 68–9
Somerset, Lord Charles 22
Sontonga, Enoch 16–17
Soros, George *see* Open Society
South African Commercial Advertiser 22–3
South African Human Rights Commission 26
South China Morning Post 104
Soviet bloc 6–7
speech, freedom of *see* freedom of expression
standards *see* professional standards
Sunday Times (South Africa) 28
Sweden 21, 80

threats *see* safety
Tiktok 56, 71
Toff, Benjamin 93
Toledano, Michael 34
Toronto Star 41
transparency 60, 63, 94
transphobia *see* gender
trust in news media *see* audiences
Trust Mark 94
truth, truthfulness xiii, 3, 29, 39, 47–9, 59, 63–5, 72–5, 110; *see also* accuracy; facts; epistemology
Turk, James (Jim) xv
Tutu, Desmond 18
Twitter 20

ubuntu 11
UNESCO 6–7, 32, 46, 75, 81, 99, 102
unions of journalists and labour issues 82, 95, 109
United Kingdom (or Britain) 22, 37, 39, 45, 51, 87, 91, 93, 112
United Nations 6, 8, 30
United States 13, 51, 67, 78, 93, 95, 99, 113
Universal Declaration of Human Rights 7, 9, 15, 30

"valuable journalism" 107
verification 54, 60, 66, 73, 87, 100
Vietnam 112
Vos, Tim 58–9

Waisbord, Silvio 49, 65
Wardle, Claire 47
Wasserman, Herman xiv
WhatsApp 56, 69
whistleblowers 22, 32
"who is a journalist?" *see* journalism and journalists
Windhoek Declaration 32, 46
Winston, Brian 20–1
Winston, Matthew 20–1

women, discrimination against 4–6, 8, 12, 99
World Conference on Human Rights 14
World Press Freedom Index *see* Reporters Without Borders (RSF)
Worlds of Journalism Study 57, 62, 84n26
Wright, Shelley 4

Yangming He 19
Yousafzai, Malala 44

Zommer, Laura 46, 56, 67–71

For Product Safety Concerns and Information please contact our EU
representative GPSR@taylorandfrancis.com
Taylor & Francis Verlag GmbH, Kaufingerstraße 24, 80331 München, Germany

www.ingramcontent.com/pod-product-compliance
Lightning Source LLC
Chambersburg PA
CBHW051748230426
43670CB00012B/2206